CODEPENDENCY RECOVERY
WORKBOOK

BOOKS BY LULU NICHOLSON

Transformative Shadow Work: Guide, Workbook & Journal—The 3-Step System to Embrace Your Hidden Self and Transcend Emotional Triggers & Past Traumas to Reduce Stress, Enhance Personal Growth, and Improve Relationships

CODEPENDENCY RECOVERY WORKBOOK

STEP-BY-STEP GUIDE TO OVERCOME FEAR OF ABANDONMENT,
STOP PEOPLE PLEASING, SET BOUNDARIES,
AND DEVELOP HEALTHY RELATIONSHIPS
BY RESTORING **SELF-WORTH** & **SELF-LOVE**

LULU NICHOLSON

Contents

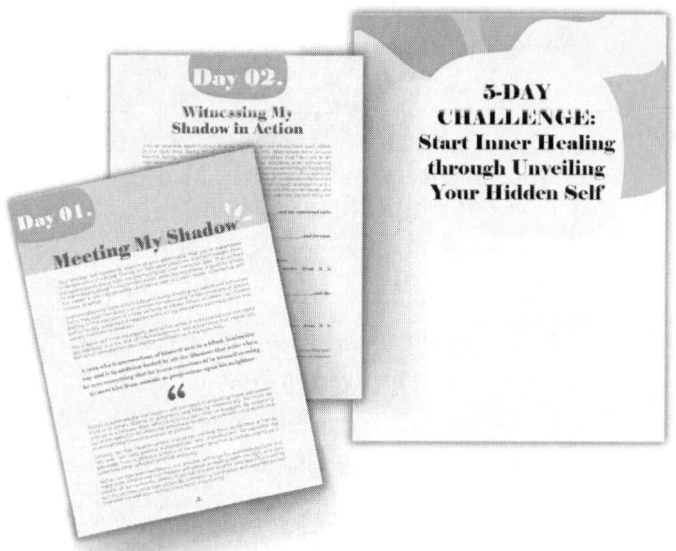

Start Inner Healing Through Unveiling Your Hidden Self.'

Simply scan the QR code and provide the email address you'd like it delivered to. This 5-day program will help you begin your self-improvement journey on the right foot:

Day 1: MEETING MY SHADOW

Day 2: WITNESSING MY SHADOW IN ACTION

Day 3: INTEGRATING MY SHADOW

Day 4: ACCEPTING MY SHADOW

Day 5: BECOMING WHOLE

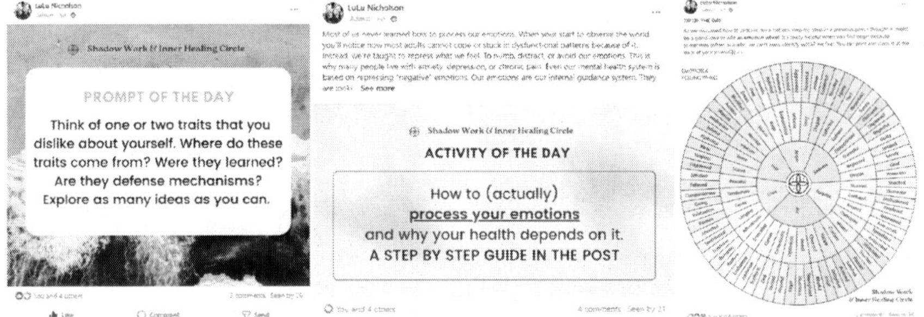

Additionally, I invite you to join the
'Shadow Work & Inner Healing Circle' Facebook Group
for Daily Prompts and Activities.

This new community is designed for beginners and those well into their journey, and it is suitable for:

- Anyone seeking to incorporate inner work into their daily routine and make it a lifelong practice.
- Anyone in search of support and accountability within a private, safe space.
- Anyone looking to connect with like-minded individuals.
- Anyone seeking tangible, practical steps and healing tools to delve deeper into their journey.
- Anyonc (and I mean anyone) seeking to create change in their life!

Introduction

There are two questions a man must ask himself: The first is "Where am I going?" and the second is "Who will go with me?" If you ever get these questions in the wrong order you are in trouble. –Sam Keen

"

Codependency or Reality?

Who is a codependent person? How do they behave? Could you point them out in a crowded room? Unlike mental health conditions like narcissism or bipolar disorder, codependency is a relationship pattern that isn't obvious to spot.

Take Kerri-Ann, a selfless stay-at-home mother who's passionate about taking care of her family. Her compulsion to serve others often leads to pushing her needs aside. When her help is rejected or undervalued, she feels a sense of inadequacy and questions whether she should've done more.

Or Michael, a highly ambitious mid-level manager who goes above and beyond expectations to gain recognition at work. On the outside, he seems like any other success-driven young man wanting to get ahead in his career. However, his obsessive need for approval is what motivates him internally. What he desires more than success is to be accepted and reaffirmed as a valuable member of the team.

Or Khadija, a single woman who hasn't experienced much luck finding true love. In relationships, she loses herself in seeking to please her romantic partners. Whatever they like, she likes it. Their strong beliefs become her strong beliefs. Under the charm and vibrant energy, Khadija suffers from a chronic feeling of not being good enough. Being in a relationship reassures her that she is capable of giving and receiving love. Outside of relationships, she feels like something in her life is missing.

Many of the behaviors mentioned above are what we would consider "normal." After all, shouldn't a mother sacrifice her momentary comfort to give her children a bright future? Isn't it expected for professionals to build a good reputation and get the thumbs up from their seniors and teammates? And when in a committed relationship, isn't it normal to develop common interests and beliefs with your significant other?

Due to the subtle nature of codependency, you may still be in denial about whether or not you have this relationship pattern. How you relate to others may not be something that raises alarm bells, even when you notice a severe decline in your mental, physical, and emotional well-being—*isn't love supposed to hurt sometimes?*

Perhaps you have always sacrificed your needs to make others happy, and this just feels like an unchangeable aspect of your personality. You may even think that you are cursed for caring so deeply about people who shamelessly walk all over you and cannot reciprocate half of the love and respect you give. Alternatively, you may feel proud of being people-focused because there aren't many virtuous people left in this world. Overgiving is something that makes you loveable to others and, therefore, not seen as a threat. *But how much does taking care of others cost you in the end?*

Who Is This Book For?

This comprehensive guide has been created for anyone interested in codependency recovery. Whether you have mild or severe symptoms of codependency, this book includes information and plenty of strategies that you can learn and practice in your relationships. Please note that the book covers all types of relationships where codependency exists, such as the parent-child relationship, intimate relationships, friendships, and professional relationships. Therefore, as you flip through the pages, you will find nuggets of wisdom that resonate with your personal experiences.

How to Use This Book

By picking up this book, you have shown a desire to learn more about codependency and the various ways it can impact your relationships. You are curious to know when and how you might have learned this pattern and whether there is hope of healing from it and adopting healthier relationship habits. On the other hand, you may be carrying emotional issues from past relationships where you were mistreated. These issues could date as far back as your early interactions with your parents to your most recent breakup.

This book will show you the connection between your emotional issues and your codependency tendencies. By healing one, you inadvertently heal the other. Some of the emotional issues that will be explored include low self-worth, people-pleasing, the fear of standing up for yourself, the fear of abandonment, and the fear of setting healthy boundaries (to name a few). Staying true to the promise of a workbook format, the book also provides actionable strategies. Each chapter includes practical exercises, reflective prompts, and tangible steps that empower you to take action and rewrite the course of your relationships and your life.

What makes this book an irreplaceable part of your healing journey is its signature "Complete You" blueprint, which teaches you how to develop a strong sense of self and advocate for your needs in relationships. The content, actionable steps, and exercises included in this book focus on igniting inner transformation that leads to long-lasting change. You can expect a holistic transformation that enhances your mental, emotional, and spiritual well-being and guides you through a journey of self-discovery that encourages a profound shift in mindset, behaviors, communication, and relationships.

This book is a product of love, written and published by a therapist-endorsed author and a life coach who is dedicated to the field of self-improvement, with a strong focus on psychology enriched with holistic principles and spiritual insights. My passion lies in guiding individuals on their path to self-discovery through my writings. I craft content centered around mental health, relationships, personal growth, and stress management. My approach blends evidence-based principles with practical exercises and relatable examples, aiming to make complex concepts accessible to my readers.

Having embarked on my transformative journey from a challenging past to a fulfilling present, I aim to write from a place of authenticity and share insights that I have learned through my exploration of consciousness and some amazing spiritual experiences I have had along the way. By the end of this book, you will have your "aha" moment, too, and go from thinking, "You complete me" to "I complete me." This life-altering shift in consciousness will help you discover that all the "missing" pieces of yourself that you search for in others can be found within.

You were always enough, but now it's time to see and experience that for yourself!

Trigger Warning

This book explores trauma and abuse that may be triggering to sensitive readers. Moreover, the strategies and suggestions offered in this book do not substitute seeking professional diagnoses and medical treatment from a licensed practitioner. The author cannot be held liable for any unpleasant circumstances you experience during and after reading this book.

01.

The Life of a Giver and Taker—Understanding the Spectrum of Codependency

We rescue people from their responsibilities. We take care of people's responsibilities for them. Later we get mad at them for what we've done. Then we feel used and sorry for ourselves. That is the pattern, the triangle. –Melody Beattie

“

Dependency, Desperation, and Despair

Codependent relationships don't raise alarm bells at the beginning. Both people idealize each other and buy into the fantasy of being soulmates. They fall in love with the idea of true love and project their wants and desires onto one another. They feel a sense of relief after searching through the disappointing dating or friendship pools and finally finding their missing puzzle piece—someone who gets them and completes the full picture of their lives.

Their first encounter is a memory that later justifies why leaving the relationship feels impossible. They feel a strong emotional connection to each other despite not having any history. It feels as though they have met before, perhaps in a previous lifetime, and therefore don't have to waste time on getting to know each other (or following the typical stages of a relationship).

In each other's presence, they feel accepted and validated. They voluntarily share deep thoughts and feelings that they wouldn't feel safe disclosing to anyone else. Being open and vulnerable with each other allows them to learn more about their past experiences and the similar traumas and emotional issues they are carrying. Not only are they connected by their strong desire to love and be loved in return, but they are also connected by the pain and suffering they have both endured. This sounds like a match made in heaven, except for the fact that both people quickly lose themselves in the relationship and go through a cycle of dependency, desperation, and despair.

Dependency is the first stage that codependent couples or friends go through. During this stage, a few lifestyle changes occur. The two most noticeable ones are spending excessive amounts of time together and being distant from friends and family. They believe that they can conquer the world without interference from other people, and in the process, they forget about the interests and hobbies they enjoyed as two singles. They develop a new culture in their relationships, which focuses on "we" and "us" and neglects "I" and "me."

Desperation, the second stage of the cycle, occurs when couples or friends believe that they cannot live without each other. The thought of losing contact or being separated (even if it means going long periods without checking on each other on the phone) triggers feelings of distress. They need access to one another at all times to feel calm and secure. Normal conflicts in their relationships create insecurity and should be avoided if possible. In their desperation to stay together, they also ignore major red flags, such as destructive habits, manipulative behaviors, and mental illness. The abusers (if any) in these relationships are not held accountable for their actions because boundaries are not enforced.

Despair, the third stage of the cycle, won't happen in every romantic relationship or friendship. However, if couples or friends reach this stage, their relationships experience irreparable damage, such as the breakdown of trust, security, and intimacy. Despair places relationships in the "Love ICU," and only professional assistance from a healthcare worker can potentially save what remains of them. The despair begins within each person through the loss of identity, depressive moods, emptiness, and dissociation from reality. After months or years, the despair seeps outward and triggers ongoing conflict, trust issues, manipulation, and resentment.

What causes the cycle of dependency, desperation, and despair is the same thing that codependent partners love and hate about each other—feeling an inexpressible and uncontrollable need for each other. It is as though an invisible umbilical cord joins them, and what feels good for one person also feels good for the other. What hurts one person also hurts the other. The fear of separation is what haunts them and creates unnecessary drama and conflict in their relationships. They hold on to each other so tightly that one or both people suffocate. They use control and manipulation tactics to prevent each other from walking away. In the end, both people feel like hostages in a toxic relationship.

Codependency Is a Spectrum

It is not easy to identify codependency traits in yourself or others because this behavioral condition exists on a spectrum. Not all codependent people approach relationships the same way and with the same tendencies. Some fall on the lower end of the spectrum and exhibit mild symptoms, while others fall on the higher end of the spectrum and exhibit severe symptoms.

Something else worth highlighting is that codependency may affect one type of relationship and not all relationships in your life. For example, you may exhibit codependency tendencies in your romantic relationships but have healthy boundaries in your friendships and professional relationships. The reason for this is that codependency is a trauma response that develops when your sense of safety has been compromised. Thus, if, as a child, you felt unsafe around your parents, you may display codependency with your children. Or if you survived an abusive intimate relationship, you may show codependency with your romantic partners.

What's also interesting to note are the extreme personality traits that manifest as a result of codependency, which range from allowing people to control you to controlling others yourself. For example, you might resonate with the "doormat" type of codependency, where you overextend yourself for others at your expense. You derive a dopamine boost by making others happy and feel inadequate when you can't be helpful or when others aren't dependent on your giving. Saying no or expressing your needs feels dangerous because of the risk of driving others away—the fear of abandonment is a constant fear at the back of your mind.

On the other hand, you may resonate with the "domineering" type of codependency, where you impose yourself on others and show a disregard for their boundaries. Your intentions for caring for and helping others may be good. For instance, you may be aware of your partner's challenges and have the skills and knowledge to help them. Or you may believe that you know what's best for your children and give unsolicited advice or make important decisions on their behalf without consulting them first (applicable to older children).

Many of the people you help can feel undermined, criticized, or judged by you, even when this wasn't your intention. For example, if you are a controlling, codependent parent, your child may feel restricted from expressing their authentic self and pressured to live up to your expectations of them. If you are a controlling, codependent partner, you may assume the role of your significant other's mother or father and treat them like a child instead of an equal.

Your intentions may be good (you simply want the best for them and believe you know what that looks like); however, unconsciously, you are molding them into someone whom you can accept rather than giving them space to learn from their mistakes, discover their interests, and become a better version of themselves. Moreover, when they don't live up to your illusions of who they can be, or when they don't show appreciation for the investment you have made in them, you may feel angry and used.

Codependent vs. Interdependent Relationships

Since codependency exists on a spectrum, it is sometimes confusing to tell the difference between healthy and unhealthy dependency on others. The first thing to note is that human beings are social creatures, requiring strong and meaningful connections to feel content, secure, and validated. The unspoken agreement in healthy relationships is that both people will work together to respond to each other's needs.

This mutual exchange of emotional labor is known as reciprocity, the balance of give-and-take. Both people take turns caring, supporting, and taking on responsibilities for one another. With that said, presenting your needs in relationships is not the same as being needy. Due to the unspoken agreement, when your friend, partner, or colleague makes requests for specific emotional needs or favors, you shouldn't feel burdened by them.

Codependency threatens the unspoken agreement and creates an unhealthy form of dependency where the bulk of the emotional labor or investment in the relationship rests on one person—YOU. No matter where you lie on the spectrum, you may struggle with the fear of showing others who you truly are and expressing what you need from them. Due to your relationship history, you may have learned that it isn't safe to rely on others to show up for you.

Perhaps you have experienced multiple failures by people and are reluctant to put your trust in them to meet your emotional needs. What has proven to keep others from disappointing you is to hide your true thoughts and feelings and become overly invested in fulfilling their needs. In other words, you are a generous giver who feels uncomfortable being on the receiving end.

This one-sided give-and-take arrangement may seem to work because you feel in control of your relationships. For as long as you stay committed to giving, you can maintain harmony in your relationships. However, beneath the surface, your unmet needs create internal conflict that makes you feel uneasy and restless. Your relationships look perfect on paper, but they don't feel satisfying. Inwardly, you hold a lot of resentment for not being seen and validated in your relationships. You may even blame others for not loving you the way you desire, even though they are unaware of your hidden needs and have failed to pick up on the hints you have thrown.

Interdependency, the opposite of codependency, provides a picture of what healthy dependency in relationships ought to look like. First and foremost, interdependent couples or friends are upfront about the type of relationship they want. They can describe what love and support mean and what they look like for them, and they can create a shared vision that they both commit to. Boundaries are also set in these types of relationships to prevent unintentional hurt. The act of honoring boundaries is in itself an expression of love because both people desire to feel safe and free to be themselves.

Another characteristic of interdependent relationships is a growth mindset. Interdependent couples or friends walk into their relationships with an open mind and a willingness to learn and grow together. They understand that for their relationships to feel fulfilling for both of them, they will need to give some and take some. Who they were and how they lived before they met could prove to be a threat to the health and stability of the relationships they are building. Thus, they are both prepared to modify their behaviors to create an emotionally safe space for each other.

How Do Codependent Relationships Start?

Codependency can manifest in different types of relationships in your life. Below is an overview of how codependency looks in romantic, familial, social, and professional relationships:

Romantic Relationships

In a romantic relationship, codependency may start with a strong desire to please your partner. Perhaps you admire several qualities about them and feel immense gratitude for the relationship. A part of you may also feel like you don't deserve to be in this relationship or receive this type of affection. You may worry that by not showing appreciation for your partner, they might realize you are not the person they want to be with.

These self-critical thoughts cause you to overextend yourself and make it your responsibility to maintain the relationship. You take on dual roles (being the provider and nurturer) and neglect your own needs and desires to make your partner happy. You perceive your needs as a burden on your partner and, therefore, do your best to hide them. You may even attempt to convince yourself that your needs don't matter or are inconvenient.

To avoid conflict or resentment (two things that you believe could sabotage your relationship), you turn a blind eye to red-flag behaviors, such as substance abuse issues, infidelity, money problems, anger issues, or emotional abuse. By excusing your partner's behavior, you believe that you are showing loyalty; however, the truth is you are enabling destructive habits that ultimately compromise the peace, safety, and intimacy in your relationship.

Family Relationships

In a family, codependency manifests as a dysfunctional family dynamic that is created by unconscious parents who don't know healthy ways to relate to each other or their children. For instance, one of your parents may have been abusive, controlling, manipulative, mentally ill, or addicted to drugs or alcohol. Their spouse (the codependent parent) became their caregiver and enabled their destructive behaviors. Your parents' tumultuous romantic relationship caused them to make several parenting oversights, which affected how they raised you.

For example, your parents may have forced you to grow up too quickly and think like an adult while you regressed and acted like a child. If you are the oldest of your siblings, you may have felt pressure to go through school and get a job so you could take care of your family. Moreover, your parents may have used manipulation to control your emotions and keep you enmeshed with them. For example, whenever you wanted someone to attend to your needs, they may have guilt-tripped you, gossiped about you, or withdrawn their attention and affection. When this felt too uncomfortable due to the fear of abandonment, you returned to focusing on your parents' needs.

Another manifestation is having an excessively controlling, codependent parent who desires to live vicariously through you. This dynamic is often seen when the codependent parent (i.e., the enabler) is married or in a partnership with an abusive or alcoholic parent (often with narcissistic tendencies). For most of their marriage or partnership, they felt obliged to take care of the abusive or alcoholic spouse, to their detriment. They sacrificed their needs, hopes, and dreams to gain approval from their partner, which unfortunately created a cycle of dependency, desperation, and despair.

The only thing your codependent parents felt they could control was you and your siblings. They could manipulate you into addressing their needs because you were dependent on them to survive—

needs that their alcoholic or abusive spouse had suppressed or neglected. In exchange for being attentive to their needs, they would offer transactional affection. In other words, if you behaved and did what they wanted, you would be rewarded with love and support. If you did something they disapproved of, they would turn cold and withdraw themselves from you.

Social Circles

A codependent friendship feels similar to a codependent romantic relationship. The two relationships start with excessive admiration and a desire for closeness. The difference is that with a codependent friendship, intimacy is replaced with emotional support and validation. This means that instead of showering your friend with affection in the romantic sense, you provide them with an unending supply of emotional support and validation.

Of course, this is not balanced. Your friend does not reciprocate the same emotional labor you provide them. However, their helplessness or need for you keeps you attached to them. Even if they are capable of taking care of themselves, making adult decisions, and solving their problems, your friend pretends to be clueless about how to take responsibility for their life and seek rescue from you. Moreover, to ensure that you continue to shower them with an endless supply of emotional support and validation, your friend may create fake problems or exaggerate their circumstances to get your attention.

Another manifestation of codependency occurs when you are friends with someone who is controlling or jealous of you. They may demand to spend a lot of time with you so that you cannot spend time with anyone else, and they may make you feel guilty on days when you prioritize your needs. They may also portray a false sense of superiority to make you feel inferior and psychologically condition you to accept their mean behaviors. Since you have placed them on a pedestal in your mind, you unconsciously tolerate behaviors that you would otherwise not. This type of friend plays on your insecurities to get you obsessed with them and desperate to maintain the friendship by providing intermittent praise (e.g., switching from validating to criticizing you).

Work Relationships

Codependency manifests at work whenever professional boundaries are blurred, and you start to treat your coworkers like you would your friends or family members. For example, you may be someone who seeks out validation from your manager and becomes upset when you aren't given the recognition you deserve. This type of behavior would be appropriate for an intimate or familial relationship where emotional support is expected. However, in the workplace, where employees are paid to complete their job duties, receiving emotional support should not be an expectation.

Another manifestation of codependency is being overly helpful and spending a lot of your time and energy nurturing your work relationships. The need to be liked by others could lead to desperate behaviors like being overly helpful, apologizing for mistakes that were not your fault, compromising your work boundaries to keep the peace, and taking on responsibilities that do not fall within your job description.

Sometimes, codependency is displayed by your manager. A common sign of this is having a manager who wants to be updated on daily tasks and included in every email. They struggle to step back and allow you to manage your time and make decisions on how to perform everyday tasks. If you are an independent person who likes to take ownership of your work, the constant reporting and needing to explain your reasoning to your manager can be frustrating. Your independence can also be interpreted as not needing your manager, which could trigger their fear of abandonment. As a means to control you, they may restrict how much work you are given, not inform you about training opportunities, or make excuses for not increasing your salary or promoting you.

The Karpman Drama Triangle

In the 1960s, psychiatrist Stephen Karpman invented the Karpman Drama Triangle, a model to illustrate the power games that people, in particular codependents and narcissists, play in dysfunctional relationships (Grace Being, 2021). The model consists of three roles: the rescuer, the persecutor, and the victim.

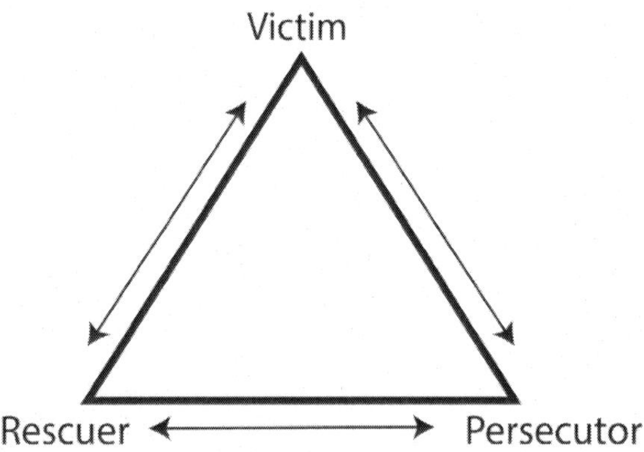

Codependents and narcissists switch between these roles depending on the nature of their circumstances and what version of themselves is needed at each moment. When one person changes roles, it automatically causes the other person to adopt a different role too. Learning how to recognize the Karpman Drama Triangle in your codependent relationships can help you identify toxic behavioral patterns when they occur and how much give-and-take (if any) happens.

Here is a breakdown of how the Karpman Drama Triangle manifests between codependents and narcissists in romantic, family, social, and work relationships:

The Rescuer

Codependent people are often seen as rescuers in relationships. They derive pleasure from fixing broken people and helping out where they can. The negative side of this behavior is that they often feel responsible for changing people or saving toxic relationships. They struggle to accept their limits and withdraw from dead-end situations.

At the beginning of relationships, usually during the love-bombing stage, narcissists can also play the role of rescuers. They go to great lengths to convince their codependent partners or friends that they are the ideal person they have been looking for. By understanding human psychology, they can create illusions around their personalities and get codependents to admire them.

The Persecutor

Narcissistic people are typically seen as persecutors. The persecution tends to start when their codependent counterparts are emotionally dependent on them for validation or support. They shift from love-bombing to devaluing their loved ones through all sorts of deception and manipulation. To maintain a positive self-concept about themselves, narcissists will blame their bullying behaviors on the shortcomings of their partners.

Codependent people can also become persecutors in relationships when they grow tired of suppressing their needs and become increasingly frustrated. It dawns on them that they have allowed their narcissistic partners or friends to walk all over them, and this revelation makes them angry. To "get even," codependents can take extreme measures like becoming uncooperative, demanding unrealistic changes, or being authoritarian (especially at work or in family situations). They go from having no boundaries to having rigid and unfair boundaries. However, despite their efforts to correct the power imbalance, they are unsuccessful at winning the narcissistic partner's respect and cooperation.

The Victim

Codependent people are commonly seen as victims whenever they are coupled with narcissistic people. Their inability to express their thoughts and feelings and advocate for their needs leaves them feeling powerless. Moreover, being emotionally dependent on their narcissistic partners or friends means that even when they are mistreated, they look to their counterparts for validation.

Narcissists will play the victim when it benefits them. For example, to avoid taking accountability for their actions, narcissistic partners or friends will turn the tables and focus on the faults of their loved ones. They may also use psychological manipulation to prey on their counterparts' insecurities and trap them in a spider web of confusion, self-doubt, and self-loathing. As a result, their counterparts start questioning their reality, like whether or not the abuse they are subjected to is true or fictional.

Leaving the Karpman Drama Triangle is never easy, especially because there is normally a trauma bond between the couple or friends. In other words, they share similar emotional wounds and have been through toxic relationship patterns in the past. The unhealthy dynamic between them often reinforces a parent-child dynamic they already know. Breaking free from this triangle requires awareness and the willingness to reprogram the mind.

For instance, the rescuer must recognize the avoidant behaviors that cause them to fixate on other people's problems as a way to escape facing their own issues. The persecutor must be willing to cultivate self-awareness and respect other people's boundaries. And finally, the victim should develop emotional intelligence and work on rediscovering who they are outside of their relationship.

Ending the Dysfunctional Cycle of Give and Take

With everything that we have covered in this chapter, the main takeaway that you can hold onto is that codependent relationships create a power imbalance where one person gives more than the other. The giver sacrifices their needs to attend to the needs of the taker, and in the process, they lose touch with who they are and what makes them happy.

What makes the power imbalance dangerous is that eventually, the giver will deplete their physical, mental, and emotional energy seeking to please and keep their partner satisfied. They may develop mental health issues and pick up unhealthy coping mechanisms to hide their pain. Moreover, as much as the giver may try desperately to save the relationship, being with someone who dismisses their needs and fails to reciprocate the affection and support they are shown will lead to the collapse of the relationship and create the following problems:

- trust issues
- lack of respect

- internalized anger and resentment
- feeling the need to lie to avoid conflict
- breakdown of communication
- trouble setting and respecting boundaries

When you discover that you are in a codependent relationship, it is not too late to seek help, either alone or with your loved one. If you are considering seeking help with your loved one, make sure that they are committed to repairing your relationship. Fixing your problems will require honesty and vulnerability from both of you, as well as the willingness to work through your relationship challenges together.

If it is not possible to seek help as a couple, don't be afraid to begin the healing process alone. Individual therapy can help you get behind your codependency tendencies, confront harmful behavioral patterns, and rediscover who you are outside of your relationship. The purpose of this book is to assist you on this healing journey by offering you simple tools that you can practice in the comfort of your home.

Codependency is a behavioral pattern that you learned earlier in your life, which informs how you show up in various relationships. By turning inward and searching for clues within, you can gain insight into how and when this pattern developed, as well as underlying emotional issues that could be reinforcing it. The next chapter will take you through the process of introspection and self-reflection, so you can understand your relationship with codependency better.

EXERCISE

What Type of Relationship Do You Have?

Earlier in the chapter, we looked at the difference between codependent and interdependent relationships. Here is a checklist of codependency and interdependency characteristics to determine what type of relationship you have:

Codependency characteristics	**Yes**	**No**
You are attracted to people who need to be rescued.		
You feel responsible for your loved one's actions or reactions.		
You sacrifice your needs to keep the peace in your relationship.		
Your moods are easily affected by your loved one's moods.		
You crave constant reassurance from your loved one to feel good about yourself.		
You feel anxious when your loved one is away, distant, or unavailable.		
You feel jealous whenever your loved one gives attention to other people, including their close friends and family members.		
Interdependency characteristics	**Yes**	**No**
You feel comfortable expressing your thoughts and feelings to your loved one.		
You regularly communicate boundaries and bring up concerns you may have.		
You have an awareness of your individual goals and relationship goals.		
You make a continual effort to communicate your needs to your loved one.		
You respect your loved one's need for space and interests outside of the relationship.		
You feel secure about the relationships your loved one has with other people in their life (e.g., relationships with friends, relatives, and coworkers).		
You support your loved one's personal growth, even if it means you need to modify your behaviors.		

02.

The Power of a Pause—Breaking Free Starts With a Moment to Take Everything In

Most of our suffering comes from resisting what is already here, particularly our feelings. All any feeling wants is to be welcomed, touched, and allowed. It wants attention. It wants kindness. –Geneen Roth

"

Letting Go and Looking Inward

Introspection, the practice of looking inward, is an essential component of codependency recovery. This is because your codependency behaviors are manifestations of the quality and state of your inner world. How many times have you been dissatisfied with failed relationships and placed all the blame on your partner, friend, or coworker? "If it wasn't for their actions," you might say, "the relationship would still be going well."

The error with shifting blame onto others is that you overlook your involvement in these failed relationships. If everybody you enter relationships with is a mirror reflection of who you believe you are and what you believe you deserve, then mistreatment or dysfunction of any kind does, to some extent, point to the personal issues that you haven't resolved.

The codependency recovery journey encourages you to hold yourself accountable for limiting beliefs, negative self-talk, past trauma, and other mental and emotional patterns that have contaminated your view and understanding of affection, intimacy, and healthy relationships. To prepare you for this journey, there are two practices that you are going to be asked to do repeatedly: letting go and looking inward.

You cannot look inward without letting go of the stories, attachments, and expectations that keep you dependent on other people or make you hold onto them so tightly, like they are your hostages. Lovingly detaching from your loved ones will not make them run away. It can only improve your relationships as you learn to respect and celebrate their individuality and personal power.

What you may not realize is that human beings, including yourself, are more resilient than you think. Our minds and bodies were built for physical and psychological survival. We all have what is known as inner strength—the willpower and courage to overcome life obstacles. Nevertheless, we can only discover our inner strength when circumstances force us to. For as long as we are dependent on others to meet our needs, there is no reason for us to look inward.

Letting go and looking inward is not only doing yourself a favor but also empowering those you love to tap into their inner strength. It is about trusting that they have the tools to rescue themselves from hardships, just as you have the tools to do the same for yourself. Adopting this mentality creates space for you and your loved ones to evolve alongside one another instead of walking the same path and tripping over each other.

The chapter will present three introspection exercises that teach you how to pause and reflect, process emotions, and regulate your nervous system with deep breathing. Make time to practice these exercises daily to prepare for the recovery strategies discussed in the succeeding chapters.

Start With a Pause

Introspection begins by physically and mentally withdrawing from others to spend time reflecting. If you are at home, find a private and quiet space, either indoors or outdoors. If you are at work, close your office door or spend a few minutes in your car. Once you have removed yourself from your external environment, you can practice self-reflection.

Self-reflection refers to seeking to understand your thoughts, emotions, beliefs, and motivations. It is about examining what you think and feel and why you hold certain perceptions about people and life in general. It is not enough to agree with every thought that comes into your mind without investigating where it comes from and how much of it is based on your personal history or current reality.

For example, it is possible to feel a strong dislike for someone with a certain annoying personality trait and feel uncomfortable whenever you are around them. However, as real and powerful as that feeling may be, it has nothing to do with the person standing in front of you. If you reflect on the feeling, you will find that it is linked to a harmful stereotype that you learned as a child. Whenever you come across someone who fits the stereotype, you are triggered to feel disgust toward them.

Self-reflection promotes taking pauses between receiving thoughts and acting upon them. During your pauses, you can be a detective and scrutinize your thoughts without taking sides. By doing this, you will recognize that your thoughts are neither good nor bad; they merely provide information about what you are experiencing at the moment. What you decide to do with the information brought about by your thoughts is determined during your pauses. For instance, you can decide to:

- reevaluate your perspectives
- identify your fears and desires
- show gratitude for your current situation
- learn from your setbacks and see failure differently
- begin the process of healing emotional wounds

So, how exactly do you practice self-reflection and structure your pauses? Fortunately, there are intentional exercises that you can perform that can help you enhance awareness and connect with your inner life, such as:

Practice Gratitude

Think deeply about what you are grateful for today or over the past month or year. Write down a list of positive experiences or people who have made you happy. If you are going through a difficult time, think about the positive aspects of your situation that have kept you going.

Practice Mindfulness Meditation

Sit in a comfortable position and close your eyes. Allow thoughts to enter your mind at a slow and controlled pace. Give yourself enough time to observe each thought without forming judgments. Acknowledge the information you are presented with and gently shift your focus to the next thought. Repeat the same process until no more thoughts enter your mind.

Practice Journaling

Write down your thoughts and feelings on paper so you can gain a deeper understanding of your experiences and identify subconscious beliefs and patterns that inform your worldview, behaviors, and interactions with others. Continue to treat your thoughts and feelings as information that can help you connect the dots between what you perceive and how you show up in the world.

Practice Self-Talk

When processing complex thoughts and emotions, speak to yourself aloud. Don't focus on sounding smart or articulating yourself. Instead, focus on creating a safe space to listen, acknowledge, and accept your thoughts and feelings. Break down your thought processes into basic ideas or beliefs that inform what you think. Ask yourself simple questions and respond to them with simple answers. Challenge your perspectives by playing the devil's advocate.

Asking questions is a big part of self-reflection because questions allow you to go beyond your comfort zone and entertain ideas and thoughts that you otherwise wouldn't have entertained before. Examples of practices that encourage asking questions are creating gratitude lists, journaling (through journal prompts), and having dialogues with yourself. Here are some self-reflection questions that you can use for any of the practices aforementioned:

- What areas of your life are you satisfied with? What areas need your attention?
- What recurring fears enter your mind? What do you believe would happen if these fears came true?
- What expectations do you impose on yourself that are heavy to carry and live up to? How far back do these expectations date?
- What do you crave from relationships that you don't believe you can provide for yourself?
- What do you find most challenging in relationships? What do you do when you are confronted with this situation?
- What types of scenarios in relationships trigger your codependency? How do you react whenever you are triggered?
- When a loved one's actions trigger you, what are you afraid to say to them? What beliefs or assumptions block you from openly sharing this message?
- Reflect on your earliest memory, avoiding conflict. What made you afraid of engaging in conflict? What consequences did you face?
- Why do you get uncomfortable receiving support or affection from others? Reflect on your earliest memory of being denied support or affection.
- Describe scenarios in relationships when your inner critic harasses you the most. Whose voice from someone in your life (or from the past) does your inner critic sound like?

Process Your Emotions

After going through the self-reflection questions, you may have noticed a lot of heavy emotions coming up. Practices like journaling are known to tap into your unconscious mind and bring unresolved emotions to the surface. This happens because, underneath the tough exterior that you may sometimes portray outwardly, there is a wounded man or woman who carries emotional baggage from the past.

Your loved ones may not be able to see the hurt written on your face, but if they pay close attention, they might be able to see that you are hurting through your codependent behaviors. Either way, it is your responsibility to give your emotions a platform to be recognized and validated. By acknowledging and processing your emotions, you can learn how to manage them more effectively and adopt healthier behavioral patterns in your close relationships.

Five steps can help you get started on processing your emotions:

Step 1: Identify the Discomfort

The first step is to acknowledge that you are feeling something, even if you can't pinpoint the exact emotion in the beginning. Start on a physical level and notice the sensations that are going through your body. For example, does your chest feel tight? Is your heart racing? These physical sensations can point to emotions that you are carrying on a psychological level. Another clue is to observe your thoughts and notice how you are speaking to yourself. Are there critical thoughts going through your mind? Do you have strong urges to draw near or away from something or someone?

Step 2: Name the Emotion

Using the information collected from the first step, label the emotion you are feeling. Labeling your emotions is important because it allows you to separate yourself from the emotion and reflect on it from a distance. Instead of identifying yourself with the emotion (e.g., I am angry), you can accept the emotion as an experience that comes and goes (e.g., I feel/felt angry). Naming the emotion is also useful when you are trying to understand how frequently you experience the emotion and where it originates.

Step 3: Look Behind the Emotion

Now that you know what emotion you are experiencing, use self-reflection tools to look behind it. Consider the fact that your emotion is a symptom of a deeper wound or experience. With curiosity and openness, explore what wound or experience that might be. For instance, could a recent event trigger you? Could your body be reacting due to an unmet need? Could you be defaulting to old behavioral patterns learned in childhood? Could one of your boundaries have been violated? Document your discoveries and read over previous journal entries to get insight into what lies beneath your emotions.

Step 4: Validate Your Emotion

Your emotion is no longer a foreign feeling in your body. You can name how you feel and describe what made you feel this way. The next step is to validate your emotions and reassure yourself that it is okay to have this type of response. Hold space for your emotion by allowing it to flow through your body without attempting to restrain it. Acknowledge the discomfort that may occur, but do your best not to identify with it. Simply observe the discomfort like you would any kind of pain or tension in your body. Holding space for your emotions symbolizes acceptance of your feelings and experiences. If you like, you can communicate this acceptance by whispering loving phrases to yourself, like "I embrace this temporary suffering. I find value in this moment."

Step 5: Release the Emotion

When attempting to understand how situations affect you or learn more about your experiences, emotions are helpful. But after gathering as much information as you can from your emotions, you must release them. Failure to safely release emotions causes them to grow and become unmanageable, or you can return to your unconscious mind and wait for the next trigger that will bring them to the surface. You can release your emotions through a simple breathing exercise:

- Take a deep breath through your nose and imagine the air clearing your mind and body of chaotic thoughts and feelings.

- As you breathe out of your mouth, imagine that all of the mental and emotional clutter is flowing out of you.

- Repeat this exercise several times, visualizing clutter being released from your mind and body until you can no longer trace your emotions.

Processing your emotions can feel unsettling, especially on your first attempt. To keep your mind and heart open to the process, it is important to be gentle with yourself and stop taking pause breaks whenever you need to. If at any point you feel like crying or screaming, don't hold yourself back. It can be difficult to predict or try to control your body's natural reactions during this process. However, rest assured that your wounds are healing the more you hold space for and embrace your emotions.

WORKSHEET

Opening Up by Writing It Down

The following worksheet consists of exercises that can help you document your experience with processing your emotions.

Writing in the Third Person

One of the ways to process your emotions without confronting them directly is to journal about how you are feeling from a third-person perspective. For example, instead of using "I" and "me," use your name and write as though you are speaking about a close friend. Practice writing in the third-person voice by describing an emotional childhood memory.

Create Emotion Personas

Construct fictional personas for your unpleasant emotions to understand them better and create enough distance between who you are and how you feel. Give your emotions humanlike qualities, such as personality, attitudes, habits, and motivations. Whenever strong emotions emerge, think of the corresponding personas and respond to them accordingly. For example, if an angry guest came into your house, how would you speak to them? What boundaries would you set? Use the lines below to create a detailed persona for a common strong emotion you experience.

Write a Poem

There are creative ways to express how you are feeling, such as by writing a poem. The great part about writing poems is that there are no formatting rules or structures that you need to adhere to. Your poem could be made of sentences, a string of words, or statements that carry significance to you. How you write about your emotions is also completely up to you. For instance, you can focus on describing the physical sensations brought on by your emotions or the thoughts that cross your mind whenever certain emotions are triggered. Use the lines below to draft a poem about an emotion you struggle to process.

Asking "So What?"

It takes several attempts to get to the root of why you feel a certain way. Your ego may prevent you from taking a deep dive into your emotions out of fear of what you might discover. For example, you might think that you feel anxious in relationships because you have trust issues. While this is somewhat true, your anxiety goes much deeper than that. If you give yourself enough time to investigate what the root issue is, you may come to a different conclusion. For instance, your anxiety could stem from fear of being abandoned, which causes you to struggle to trust how genuine other people are.

To get down to the root of your emotions, ask yourself a series of "So what?" questions. Start by making a statement about why you feel a certain way and ask at least three (or more) questions to go deeper. By the third "So what?" question, you will be able to uncover the underlying belief that you hold. Here is an example:

Statement: I am upset with my partner for not texting me promptly.

So what: So that shows me that they don't care about how I feel.

So what: So that makes me feel insignificant, and that is not fair.

So what: So that means that I am not valued in this relationship.

____

____

____

____

____

____

____

Breathe in Acceptance

You have learned how to reflect on your experiences and process strong emotions. The final introspection exercise to learn is how to self-soothe and accept how you feel. It is common for codependent people to suppress or deny their emotions due to feeling guilty or ashamed of them. As a child, you may have been mocked, bullied, or punished for expressing how you feel to others, which caused you to hide your feelings. Since you are working toward reconnecting with your emotions, it is important to practice allowing strong emotions to surface without resisting them.

Mindful breathing exercises help you stay inside your body and avoid drifting into your mind. Whenever strong emotions surface, you can anchor yourself in the present moment by taking deep and intentional breaths. This keeps your mind clear and your attention fixed on what you are sensing or noticing, both inwardly and outwardly.

A simple mindful breathing exercise to practice is focusing on your breaths. Notice the pace, rhythm, depth, and breadth of your breathing. Notice how deeply your breath travels in your body and the rise and fall of your belly. Your mind will be tempted to wander and entertain a passing thought. When you recognize this happening, gently shift your focus back to your breathing.

The purpose of this exercise is to anchor yourself in the present moment so you can embrace your emotions. After taking some deep breaths, reflect on what you wrote down in the Opening Up by Writing It Down worksheet. Thinking back on the exercises may trigger emotions. Remember to keep yourself anchored to the present moment by taking deep breaths. Find a phrase or affirmation that you can repeat to yourself that shows acceptance of your emotions or willingness to change. For example, "I will stand up for myself."

This chapter is intended to teach you how to reflect on your experiences and nurture your emotions as you proceed on the codependency recovery journey. You are now ready to learn the signature "Complete You" blueprint that will transform the intimate relationship you have with yourself and others.

A Guided Journey to the Complete You

There's only one thing that makes someone change: their own realization that they need to do it. And there's only one time it will happen: When they decide they're ready. –Lori Deschene

When we search for friends or romantic partners, we often look for people who can make us feel complete within ourselves. Part of the motivation for this is to find people who can fill our inner emptiness and make us feel alive or cherished. The media and romance novels have duped us into believing that self-love is something that we can outsource to others. Therefore, we tend to enter relationships with the expectation that our friends or partners are responsible for helping us heal from past hurts.

While it is possible to find people whose characters and unconditional love for us inspire us to heal, the motivation, willpower, and commitment to healing come from within. In other words, even if we are lucky enough to find our soulmates, they can never complete us. They can only mirror back to us how much healing we have done on our own and areas where we are still struggling. Healthy partnerships support us in our weaknesses and create space for us to develop and believe in our strengths.

Self-love and achieving wholeness are inside jobs that you are responsible for. There is no amount of external validation or affection from others that can make you genuinely love and celebrate yourself. The "Complete You" blueprint, which will be discussed and unpacked in the succeeding chapters, will help you address childhood fears, negative beliefs, and harmful coping mechanisms that keep you stuck in cycles of self-sacrificing in exchange for being seen, respected, and accepted by others.

The blueprint will also help you take back the power you have given others to dictate how you feel about yourself and how much love you deserve. You will be empowered to let go of relationships that trigger your emotional wounds and make you feel unsafe and be courageous enough to build and nurture relationships that honor your needs, align with your values, and bring out the secure and authentic version of you!

03.

The Thin Line Between Caregiver and Enabler—How to Care Without Losing Yourself in the Process

I used to spend so much time reacting and responding to everyone else that my life had no direction. Other people's lives, problems, and wants set the course for my life. Once I realized it was okay for me to think about and identify what I wanted, remarkable things began to take place in my life. –Melody Beattie

"

Caregiver vs. Enabler

A caregiver is someone who cares for or provides support to others. In professions like nursing, teaching, or elderly support, caregiving is a paid service. However, in familial, social, or romantic relationships, caregiving is treated as emotional labor. The role of caregiver is assigned to the partner, who is a natural nurturer. In some relationships, it is the female partner, and in others, it is the male partner.

Being a caregiver is not a weakness. It simply means that you are attentive and empathetic to other people's needs and find pleasure in playing a supportive role. There is a lot of value that you bring to your relationships, such as being intuitive, patient, compassionate, and dependable. The difference between healthy caregiving and caregiving that leads to codependency is the presence or absence of boundaries.

Knowing your limits and being able to say no can ensure that your passion for taking care of loved ones doesn't compromise your well-being or turn you into an enabler. An enabler is someone who does not hold their loved one accountable for their actions. They allow all kinds of behaviors to occur without speaking against them or drawing boundaries.

Some of these behaviors could be self-destructive, such as an enabler watching their partner's drinking problem become worse without intervening. Other behaviors negatively impact the enabler, such as the alcoholic partner verbally or emotionally abusing the enabler without them being held accountable for their actions.

Enabling can sometimes look like being supportive even though it isn't. For example, an enabling mother will nurture her grown child and protect them from facing adult challenges and responsibilities. In her eyes, she is doing what every loving mother should do—provide a safe and supportive environment for her child. What she may not realize is that by continuing to "mother" a grown child, she is making it more difficult for them to complete their stage of individuation (typically started in adolescence), where the teenage child develops a separate identity from their parents and becomes independent.

To determine whether you are a caregiver or enabler, ask yourself whether you are capable of saying no to your loved ones or calling out destructive behaviors. Moreover, consider how you feel when you are helping others. For instance, do you feel pleasure when doing things for others, or do you see your duties as obligations? Do you feel liberated or trapped in the caregiver role?

Four Stages of Enabling

Another way to understand enabling is to learn how this relational pattern develops over time. Consider the four stages of enabling and reflect on how some or all of these behaviors manifest in your relationships:

Stage 1: Denial

The act of turning a blind eye to someone's bad behavior carries with it a lot of shame. As an adult, you are aware of acceptable and unacceptable behaviors and know when someone has violated your boundaries. However, unlike other people, you find it difficult to speak out against unacceptable behaviors. To hide your shame, you may deny the severity of your loved one's actions or make excuses for them. Denying and downplaying their unacceptable behaviors makes you feel less pressured to take action against them.

Stage 2: Compliance

In the long run, denial turns into compliance with destructive behaviors. Compliance means maintaining the rules or standards of something. Thus, as an enabler, you become so accustomed to the mistreatment or acts of self-destructive habits of your loved one that they become normalized in your relationship. You may even start to believe that your loved one's destructive behaviors are part of their personality and cannot be undone.

Stage 3: Control

The silent dysfunction in your relationship becomes so obvious that you cannot deny it anymore. This is when you will seek control over the dysfunctional situation. Like any enabler, you believe that you are responsible for fixing (or at least hiding) the dysfunction. You take it upon yourself to manage your loved one's compromised social reputation and resolve problems that have been created by their poor choices of behavior. For example, you might bail your loved one out of jail after they have been arrested for a DUI, lend them money to pay off loans, take over their bills, or attempt to salvage relationships that they have ruined.

Stage 4: Crisis

Eventually, the issues in your relationship will become too large for you to manage on your own. Without the physical, mental, emotional, and financial support of your loved one, you run out of strength to attend to every crisis. Despite all of the turmoil unfolding around you, you may still feel a sense of loyalty to your partner and vow to stay with them to work on your relationship. Nevertheless, your loved one's blindness or lack of accountability for their actions makes it difficult for you to work together to bring about effective changes. As a result, your health and relationship continue to deteriorate until you decide to break free from the codependent cycle.

It is worth emphasizing that enabling comes with shame and can be hard to speak openly about. If you are an enabler, you feel ashamed for tolerating your loved one's behaviors when you are aware that they are wrong. Deep down, you know that you shouldn't be accepting those kinds of behaviors or staying in toxic relationships. However, you are also aware of the consequences of speaking out and setting boundaries, especially if you are in a relationship with a narcissistic person. For example, you may be afraid that in their narcissistic rage, they could become aggressive, verbally attack you, or punish you with silent treatment or other forms of manipulation.

The four stages of enabling can continue in a cycle for years and even decades. Freeing yourself from this toxic dynamic requires choosing to advocate for your needs without discounting the needs of your loved ones. However, your first and only course of action is to choose yourself when their needs conflict with yours or when they ignore your needs.

The Thin Line Between Caring for Others and Yourself

It is important to state once again that caring for others is not a weakness. If you are an empath or altruistic person, you are naturally drawn to helping and encouraging other people. But with that said, not everybody sees the world in the same way you do. You may have close friends, relatives, or colleagues who are self-centered and cannot see past their own needs and comforts. These people are not driven to help or support others. When they come across individuals like you, they think of ways to benefit from your generosity or open heart and will shamelessly drain your energy until you have nothing left for yourself.

Although your caregiving is a positive quality, you must be willing to set boundaries with people and manage how much time and energy you invest in others. Setting healthy boundaries will protect you from overextending yourself to the point of burnout or being the only person in a one-sided relationship. The following strategies will help you address enabling tendencies and create healthy boundaries in your romantic, familial, social, and professional relationships.

Strategy 1: Allow Natural Consequences

Natural consequences are controlled by the universal law of cause and effect. According to the law, every action has an equal reaction or consequence. If you act improperly, you will face negative consequences for your actions. Whenever you notice your loved one taking actions that are risky or destructive, resist the urge to step in and offer advice or clean up their mess. When you intervene, they miss an opportunity to be held accountable for their actions. Allow the universe to teach your loved one important life lessons by stepping back and allowing natural consequences.

Here's how this strategy applies in various relationships:

Romantic

Think of how you step in to rescue your partner from facing the consequences of their actions. How do you feel inside your body when your partner is making bad decisions? The next time you feel an impulse to rescue your partner, take a few deep breaths, tune into your body, and connect with how you feel. Journal about your fears and anxieties, talk yourself out of playing the role of savior, and see the benefit of your partner learning from their mistakes.

Family

Do you often make excuses for your family members or take on more responsibility than you should because that is what you were conditioned to believe is unconditional love? Allowing natural consequences simply means stepping back and creating room for the universe to naturally correct the order of things. You don't need to speak out against your family members to ensure they are held accountable for their actions. You simply need to stop trying to fix or change them or go into damage control whenever they get themselves into trouble.

Social

In social circles, it is common to find friends who expect you to give more than they do to sustain the friendships. For instance, they might reach out to you whenever they need emotional support but disappear when they are stable and regulated. In these situations, allowing natural consequences means letting these friendships take the natural course. For example, when your friend stops communicating with you, the natural course of action is for the friendship to fizzle out. If your friend doesn't offer support to you, the natural course of action is to quit making yourself available for support, too.

Professional

At work, you desire to get ahead and succeed. However, your success shouldn't compromise your values or boundaries. To resist the urge to become a people-pleaser, be clear about your duties and responsibilities. Study your company's policies and codes to know your rights. Whenever you are treated improperly, refer to your rights as an employee or employer. When asked to "cover" for others or do unethical favors, consider the natural consequences that come with those requests. Ask yourself if you really want to be held liable for someone else's poor choices. If not, politely decline to assist.

Strategy 2: Establish Boundaries

Remind yourself daily that you are not responsible for other people's thoughts, feelings, desires, and behaviors. Their actions are a result of their choices. Likewise, no one is responsible for your thoughts, feelings, desires, or behaviors. How you act is based on the choices you make. Thus, when you sacrifice your needs to please others and hurt yourself in the process, you are deliberately putting yourself down. *Is this the type of relationship you want to have with yourself?*

Boundaries cut off your energetic supply from people who constantly take from you without giving back. They create healthy limits so that your caregiving doesn't negatively impact your well-being. When you establish boundaries, you can maintain your supportive role but do so within set parameters. In other words, for the sake of your peace of mind, there are certain favors, requests, or behaviors that you cannot fulfill.

Here's how this strategy applies in various relationships:

Romantic

As a natural caregiver, you have a lot of compassion for other people's needs. In your romantic relationship, this may cause you to agree to fulfill needs that make you feel uncomfortable. For example, you might agree to take on duties that go against your principles just because you understand the significance of these duties to your partner. It is important to remember that what matters to your partner doesn't necessarily have to become important to you. With open communication and compromise, you can meet in the middle and find ways to merge your individual beliefs and expectations without overlooking your principles. A simple way to communicate this is by saying, "I respect your need for this... I am comfortable with... I am uncomfortable with... can we meet in the middle?"

Family

In codependent families, it is common to find family members who are enmeshed with each other, meaning that there are no boundaries between them or distinction of roles. For example, parents can become so involved in their children's lives that they act like close friends or even romantic partners (without the sexual acts). If you come from a family like this, establishing boundaries can help you create a healthy separation from your family so you can mature, learn to think for yourself, and grow into your own person. The most important boundaries when dealing with enmeshment are those related to privacy, personal space, time, and communication. Consider how involved you want your family members to be in different aspects of your life and how much information you share with them.

Social

In friendships, support and validation are very important needs, regardless of how they are given. When you do not feel supported or validated, or when you are giving more support and validation than your counterpart, a boundary needs to be established. It is not always necessary to verbally communicate your boundaries with friends (unlike in romantic partnerships or family relationships, where communication is vital). Instead, you can set boundaries through your actions. For example, when your friend doesn't make time for you, slowly decenter them from your life and withdraw your attention. This type of action speaks louder than words. It shows them that unless they make you a priority, you will not continue to make them a priority, either.

Professional

Work boundaries are essential in the workplace to maintain healthy and professional relationships. Remember that your work colleagues are not your friends or family members, which means that how you interact with them needs to be different. Work boundaries create distance between you and colleagues so you can stay focused on shared goals and work tasks without getting your emotions or personal lives involved. Your work boundaries can regulate how you spend your time, communicate with others, structure your work day, organize your workstation, and respond to requests that fall outside of your billable hours or work expectations.

Strategy 3: Focus on Your Life

To avoid enabling and getting stuck in the rescuing role, spend more of your time working on personal goals and improving your standard of living. Respect your loved ones enough to allow them to make decisions about their lives. This is what is meant by putting your needs first. When your needs are your number one priority, your physical, mental, and emotional well-being are always on your mind. You become attuned to your body and can pick up on slight changes in your moods, health, and behaviors. This level of focus on yourself helps you address mental, emotional, and physical problems as they arise instead of waiting until they become big and unmanageable. It is also a great reminder that you are human, too, and deserve affection and nurturing.

Here's how this strategy applies in various relationships:

Romantic

Being in a romantic relationship doesn't mean that you should forget who you are as an individual. While you may have a lot in common with your partner, there are still personal interests or hobbies that they may not understand or find particularly interesting. Maintain your individuality by making time to explore these interests and hobbies by yourself. This isn't about shutting your partner out of a certain area of your life. It is about continuing to pursue personal growth while in a committed, long-term relationship. Plus, when you enjoy experiences as an individual, you have so much knowledge or many interesting stories to share with your partner that can make your conversations fun and insightful.

Family

Do you have family members who are mentally ill or suffering from an addiction? Are you normally the peacekeeper at home who manages conflict between family members? Having to constantly take care of sick family members or mediate disputes can be exhausting. Moreover, it consumes a lot of your time and distracts you from your personal goals and relationships. A great way to start focusing on your life is to become too busy to focus on anyone else's. Start filling up your calendar with personal tasks or social events to limit the time spent on family matters. Have a rule for how much contact you have with your family. For example, instead of spending the whole weekend with them, you could see them on Sundays and spend the rest of the weekend prioritizing your needs.

Social

Do you have controlling friends who demand a lot of your time or expect you to conform to their lifestyle standards to maintain friendships? Being friends with someone or part of a friendship group shouldn't cause you to forget about your needs. Boundaries can help you manage how much time and energy you invest in your friendships. For example, you could make a rule to see your friends twice or three times a month. You can also turn down invitations to events that don't align with your needs or lifestyle preferences. If you come back home tired from work, you might decline an invitation to go out so you can spend the evening unwinding.

Professional

Your career is only a portion of your life and shouldn't become the center of your life. To manage stress and achieve a healthy work-life balance, show interest in other areas of your life, such as your social life, romantic life, physical health, hobbies and leisure activities, spirituality, and so on. Create goals for these different aspects of your life and work on them during your free time. If your work continues to infiltrate your personal life (e.g., working until the late hours of the night), you may want to consider setting stricter work boundaries for yourself and colleagues.

EXERCISE

The True Essence of a Caregiver Checklist

The energy of a caregiver is different from the energy of an enabler. While both people may look after their loved ones, they show up differently in their relationships. Caregivers have a loving and inviting aura. They are sensitive to the needs of others and naturally find themselves extending kindness.

Enablers also help others, but not out of genuine concern or kindness. They feel forced to play a supportive role to make others happy or prevent loved ones from abandoning them. If it were up to enablers, they wouldn't be doing as much as they do for other people. Their aura is heavy and intense even when they are silent due to the inner conflict raging within.

If you are an enabler who was once a cheerful and passionate caregiver, there is hope for you to return to your true essence. By being more aware of your thoughts, emotions, and motivations, you can challenge limiting beliefs and work on setting healthy boundaries to manage your behaviors. Remember, unless you are giving from a place of abundance, you are depleting your energy source. Therefore, everything you do for others should come from the abundance of your heart, not the scarcity of your heart.

To remind you of the gift of being a caregiver and some of the behaviors you can aspire to, go through the following checklist:

Questions	Yes	No	Sometimes
Do you care for your loved one using their love language?			
Do you consider what your loved one truly wants before offering help?			
Can you tell what your loved one is feeling by observing their body language?			

Do you know what to do or say to make your loved one feel good about themselves?			
Are you able to notice when you are stressed and take a moment for yourself?			
Is caring for others an extension of your personality rather than a job?			
Do you find pleasure in being of service to your loved one?			
Do you respect your loved one's boundaries and step back whenever you need to?			
Do you prioritize self-care and taking as much rest as you need without feeling guilty?			
Do you pay attention to bids for affection and show love without being asked or begged?			
Does being of service to others make you feel a sense of purpose?			

When practiced within healthy boundaries, caregiving can be a beautiful quality in relationships. However, the lack of boundaries causes caregiving to turn into enabling, an unhealthy form of giving that condones destructive behaviors. If you identify as an enabler, you are likely exhausted and resentful for overextending yourself to loved ones. Caring for others may feel more like an obligation than an act of service. To return to healthy caregiving, it is important to prioritize your well-being and make sure your needs are attended to first. This will ensure that you are giving from a place of abundance, not scarcity. The next chapter continues to unpack the Complete You blueprint by exploring the overarching fear of abandonment that is at the core of codependency behaviors.

04.

Beyond the Fear of Being Left Behind—How to Overcome the Fear of Abandonment

The less you cling to something, the less fear you have of losing that something or someone. The less fear you have, the more love you have. It is true that you love even more when you let go of the need for it. Love grows when grief goes. Make your love stronger than your fear.
–Kate McGahan

"

Nobody Wants to Be Alone

David was raised in a conservative family by an authoritarian father and a subservient mother. He was fortunate to come from a two-parent household; however, his relationship with his parents was less than ideal.

His father was a traditional man with an old-school approach to raising him and his brothers. He emphasized achievement and displaying toughness but rarely, if ever, showed emotional support. Displays of masculine strength would be rewarded with praise and what felt like affection (later on, David discovered this was validation). However, "unmanly" or irresponsible behaviors would be punished with coldness and criticism.

David's mother, a traditional woman who feared her husband, enabled the harsh discipline received by her children at the hands of their father. She knew that her husband's parenting style was harming her children but downplayed the severity of it in her mind. Instead of standing up for her children, she protected her husband by echoing everything he said and did. Whenever he would praise the boys, she would praise the boys. But when he would violently attack the boys, she would be angry and dismissive, too.

David developed an anxious attachment to his parents due to being conditioned to expect hot and cold treatment from them. When he acted according to their wishes, he would receive love, but when he made decisions out of his free will or when he failed at something, his parents would turn their backs on him. This is how he developed an abandonment wound, which later complicated his adult romantic relationships.

Romantic relationships brought a lot of anxiety to David. He was a hopeless romantic who craved true intimacy but would somehow attract partners who were emotionally unavailable, demanding, judgmental, and tough to please. He enjoyed the challenge of fixing broken people or winning people over with his affection. As a result, his romantic relationships followed the same unhealthy hot and cold pattern he endured with his parents.

After several decades of failed relationships, David stopped believing in true love. For him, the best thing that a romantic relationship could offer was stability. Throughout his life, he has felt ignored, neglected, and left to figure things out on his own. Having a romantic partner in his life meant that he never had to be alone again. However, due to his abandonment wound, David always felt insecure about his relationships and feared being rejected or left behind. Many times, this became a self-fulfilling prophecy (something he unconsciously manifested) because of his attachment trauma and the type of women (i.e., emotionally unavailable and dismissive) that he would go for.

Through therapy, David eventually addressed the core abandonment wound that had developed in his childhood. He discovered that this wound was responsible for the shame and self-doubt he had felt for many years. Deep down, he didn't believe that he was worth the type of unconditional love he so desired, which is why he always settled for partners who would offer breadcrumbs. Giving so much of himself to romantic partners who were entitled and never satisfied with him reinforced the disapproval he felt from his parents. His self-love and self-esteem were negatively impacted as a child, and since then, he has searched for validation from others.

The Fear of Being Abandoned

The fear of abandonment is a deep-rooted fear of being deserted by the people you care about the most. This fear stems from traumatic childhood experiences or past relationships where you felt emotionally distressed. Due to your inability to process the trauma at the time, you developed an overwhelming fear of being hurt or neglected by people. Subsequently, you have built high walls to guard your heart against experiencing the same kind of pain in the future.

How the fear of abandonment manifests is different for everybody. It may develop as a result of physical separation from your parents, the sudden death of a parent, or experiencing emotional neglect or disconnect from your parents. In adulthood, the fear of abandonment tends to occur after a bad breakup or divorce, separation from your children, the sudden death of a spouse or child, or staying in an abusive relationship. These experiences make you feel vulnerable and exposed in the worst way, which creates fear of opening up your heart and being wounded by someone you care about.

The symptoms of the fear of abandonment can range from person to person. What is common across the board, however, is the simultaneous desire and avoidance of intimacy, which creates stress and anxiety in relationships. Here are some signs to look out for:

- being sensitive to criticism
- difficulty trusting people's intentions
- needing constant reassurance
- working hard to gain approval from loved ones
- blaming yourself when people disappoint you
- pulling back when you feel vulnerable in relationships
- sabotaging your relationships to avoid being hurt
- being afraid to leave unhealthy relationships
- avoidance of commitment or rushing into relationships
- feeling anxious when you are away from your loved ones
- difficulty going beyond the surface level in relationships

Abandonment wounds can also stem from attachment trauma. An attachment is a bond between you and your parents that begins inside the womb and becomes stronger through physical touch, nurturing, and emotional responsiveness outside of the womb. When you were an infant or small child, you couldn't fend for yourself. You needed your parents for survival. Thus, for you, attachment was equivalent to love. If your needs were taken care of and the environment you lived in felt safe and predictable, you developed a secure attachment to your parents.

A secure attachment is the ideal bond between parents and children. In this type of attachment, parents provide consistent affection and nurturing, which allows their children to feel calm and emotionally regulated. This parent-child bond feels like healthy love to children because it is reassuring and trustworthy. It doesn't blow hot and cold or feel punishing. As a result, children raised with a secure attachment tend to develop a strong sense of self-worth that enables them to build meaningful relationships and set healthy boundaries with others.

In contrast, if you are an adult who carries an abandonment wound, you are likely to live with attachment trauma contracted at some stage in your childhood. The trauma manifested during a time or season when your parent-child bond induced stress and anxiety. Due to the instability at home, you were unable to relax and play like other children raised in secure environments would.

Your fear of abandonment could be based on three unhealthy attachment styles: anxious, avoidant, or disorganized attachment. The following is a breakdown of each attachment style and how it might have impacted your sense of safety as a child.

Anxious Attachment

Anxious attachment develops when your sense of safety is threatened as a child through abuse, separation, emotional neglect, or harsh living conditions. Your parents responded to your needs sometimes but not all of the time, which caused stress and anxiety. For example, you may have been given food and shelter but were not picked up when you cried or given emotional support when you were struggling to cope. The rules at home may have been confusing, harsh, or unpredictable (e.g., you were expected to follow random rules each time).

As a young child, you soon realized that your parents were unreliable or too preoccupied with their own lives to care for you. Yes, at times, they showed you affection, but it was spontaneous and nothing that you could depend on. Your parents may not have been intentionally trying to invalidate you; they may have been living with trauma or an undiagnosed mental illness. However, their push-and-pull behavior made you afraid of trusting others, being vulnerable, and developing emotional connections.

Whenever you enter a romantic relationship or start a new friendship, you fear that at some point your partner or friend will switch up on you the same way your parents did. You become sensitive to slight changes in their behaviors or signs of rejection, and you distance yourself before you can get hurt. Since being vulnerable felt dangerous as a child, you may struggle to communicate your feelings openly with others, which makes it difficult to address and resolve conflict. You may also stay longer than you should when a relationship becomes toxic out of fear of never finding someone who genuinely cares for you again. To prevent your partner or friend from leaving you, you may become clingy or controlling.

Avoidant Attachment

Avoidant attachment develops when you have been severely traumatized as a child and decide to emotionally distance yourself from others. Unlike someone with anxious attachment who desires intimacy even though they are afraid of it, you avoid emotional closeness and depending on others. The thought of opening up to someone and receiving love is unappealing to you because, in your opinion, people cannot be trusted.

Despite your negative perceptions of others, you may still choose to find romantic love and maintain relationships with friends and family. However, what you desire is not intimacy but the illusion of it. You may be a hyper-independent person, but you still find that, at times, you feel lonely due to your abandonment wound. You are in love with the idea of romance and partnership, but you pull away or shut down whenever you are required to open up.

In romantic relationships, in particular, you tend to go for emotionally unavailable partners who have intimacy and commitment issues like yourself. Being with these types of partners feels safe because neither of you demands vulnerability. You may lovebomb each other and go through cycles of pulling and pushing each other away, and this may feel normal to both of you because of your past traumas. Furthermore, you can develop trauma bonds with your romantic partners, friends, and family, whereby your destructive habits and insecurities keep you connected in what feels like "true love."

Disorganized Attachment

Disorganized attachment is a combination of anxious and avoidant behaviors. It also develops as a result of severe childhood trauma and neglect. As a child, you may have suffered emotional distress that nobody noticed or responded to. In the absence of support and parental guidance, you were forced to soothe yourself. For this reason, everything that you know about the world or relationships is confusing because it is the culmination of different ideas and beliefs. Subsequently, you may lack a stable self-concept that informs who you are and what you want in life and in relationships.

Since disorganized attachment oscillates between anxious and avoidant tendencies, you may desire intimacy and closeness but feel unsettled in relationships. For example, you might feel a strong connection with someone but struggle to let your guard down. Or, when you are ready to commit to someone, you get the thought that something is missing. All of this stems from not having a stable sense of self. Due to your own insecurities and inner emptiness, nothing is ever certain in your life. Everything is touch-and-go.

You constantly doubt yourself and others and enjoy the chase that comes with new relationships more than seeking true commitment. When your fear of abandonment is triggered, you tend to overreact or take extreme measures, like breaking up with your partner. You may even go from being obsessed with your partner to hating them when they trigger your emotional wounds. Once again, this happens because there isn't enough of a solid foundation within yourself to self-reflect, regulate your emotions, and maturely navigate conflict. Your inner child feels stuck and confused about your past trauma and tends to emotionally explode whenever they feel unsafe in adult relationships.

Overcoming Your Fear of Abandonment

An abandonment wound can be healed using the appropriate interventions. But before you can address your wound, it is important to acknowledge where it originated. Reflect on your earliest memory of being afraid to be rejected, neglected, misunderstood, or left behind. How old were you? Who brought about this fear? What did you believe was at stake? How did this moment threaten your sense of safety?

For many people, the fear of abandonment will originate from attachment trauma or childhood emotional neglect. However, it can also come from experiencing extreme bullying, social rejection, public humiliation, or being involved in abusive romantic relationships. Furthermore, there could be many instances in your life when you felt abandoned by different people, which have all contributed to your trust, intimacy, and codependency issues.

Your anxious feelings toward relationships feed and maintain the fear of abandonment. The moment you feel uncomfortable with someone, whether they did something to make you uncomfortable or not, you respond by either pulling away (i.e., avoidant attachment) or pressing into the relationship (i.e., anxious attachment). These are both anxiety-based coping strategies that help you feel less fearful of the unknown.

Keep in mind that frequently, rather than actual proof of something happening, the thought of something happening—like the thought of your partner cheating or losing interest in you—triggers your fear of abandonment. This means that the anxiety that comes over you is not always a reliable sign of what you are experiencing in your relationship. In many cases, it is an overreaction to something that happened in previous relationships.

Overcoming your fear of abandonment involves finding healthy ways to manage your flare-ups of anxiety in relationships, so you can pause, pay attention to your thoughts and emotions, and reassess whether your safety is truly threatened or your abandonment wound has been triggered. Here are strategies to help you get started:

Seek Therapy

The most effective way to overcome the fear of abandonment permanently is to seek therapy. While at-home self-help can help you manage symptoms like anxiety, professional therapy can assist you with processing and healing from childhood trauma, as well as other emotional issues that have occurred in your life that have made you feel anxious about relationships. There are a variety of therapies that can address abandonment wounds, such as dialectical behavioral therapy (DBT), cognitive behavioral therapy (CBT), attachment-based therapy, and psychodynamic therapy (Madeson, 2023).

Focus on Self-Discovery

Show an interest in your upbringing and past experiences. Doing this can help you connect the dots between your past and present and help you understand why you approach relationships the way you do. Self-discovery is about asking yourself open and honest questions to get to know yourself better. Therefore, the best way to practice self-discovery is by talking or writing about yourself. For instance, identify someone in your life whom you trust and who is a good listener. Arrange for a time to sit down with them and share a memory about your past relationships. Another way to practice self-discovery is by journaling about your thoughts and feelings.

Soothe Your Inner Child With Self-Compassion

It is common to be triggered by your partner or friends when you are living with an abandonment wound. When this happens, think of it as your inner child warning you of potential danger. After assessing the situation and realizing that you are triggered and there isn't any real threat, reassure your inner child that you are safe. You can do this by practicing self-compassion, which involves nursing your feelings, acknowledging the discomfort, reciting affirmations, visualizing your inner child being comforted, listening to and responding to your unmet needs, and setting boundaries to prevent being exposed to the same trigger again. Anything to get you out of survival mode and feeling balanced.

Don't Take Your Feelings as Facts

Feelings are useful when you are seeking to understand how you have been impacted by a situation. However, your emotional impact does not always match the facts of the situation. This doesn't mean that your feelings are wrong or unacceptable. It simply means that you need to acknowledge and validate your feelings alongside the truth of what is happening. For example, whenever your abandonment wound is triggered, process your emotions first.

Once you are feeling calm and balanced, consider the context of your emotions. Where do they come from? What motivated those particular emotions? Did you overreact or respond appropriately to the scenario? What information did you overlook or dismiss? Would someone else in your position react similarly or differently? These self-reflection questions allow you to create enough distance between yourself and your emotions so you can assess the situation from different perspectives.

EXERCISE

Why I Fear Abandonment

To explore your fear of abandonment, select a past relationship that triggered this fear and respond to the following journal prompts (Grant, n.d.):

1. What happened in this particular relationship to make you fear being abandoned? How did this person make you feel unsafe in the relationship?

___

___

___

___

___

2. What assumptions did you make in your mind when this situation occurred? What did you tell yourself?

___

___

___

___

___

3. How did you feel believing that you were unsafe in the relationship? How did your feelings toward the other person change?

4. How did you decide to cope as a result of feeling abandoned? What were your coping strategies?

5. What habits have you adopted to prevent yourself from being vulnerable and hurt by others again? How do these habits work for you and against you?

The fear of abandonment is a sign that your sense of safety and, subsequently, trust have been compromised. This explains why you feel exposed or uncomfortable in close relationships and feel the need to cling to your loved ones tightly whenever they start to pull away. The thought of your partner, friends, or family members being physically or emotionally distant or deciding to walk away from you fills you with anxiety.

The good news is that you can overcome your fear of abandonment by learning healthy ways of managing your anxiety and acknowledging your childhood and attachment trauma. The following chapter will explore another common dynamic in codependent relationships, which is the tendency to seek approval from others.

05.

Pleasing the Self With Internal Validation—How to Stop People-Pleasing

The only thing wrong with trying to please everyone is that there's always at least one person who will remain unhappy. You.
–Elizabeth Parker

"

The Need for External Validation

One of the symptoms of codependency is people-pleasing. This behavior is characterized by looking to others to validate your thoughts, feelings, and motivations. Not every individual on the spectrum of codependency will struggle with people-pleasing tendencies. Whether you do or don't depends on how much time you have spent developing a strong sense of self.

Turning to others for validation means that, to some degree, you care about what people think about you more than the truth of what you think and feel about yourself. Perhaps you take pride in your self-image and put forth a lot of effort to influence others' perceptions of you. In your family, you may want to be perceived as the peacemaker who brings people together, which means that maintaining an image of being neutral and accepting of everyone is important to you. At work, you may want to be perceived as a dedicated employee, which means you struggle to turn down work requests.

A positive self-image is important to build and maintain, especially when you want to get ahead in your career or master the art of social networking. But with that said, how others perceive you should ideally align with your authentic self to avoid identity confusion. For example, being perceived as a peacemaker when that is genuinely how you feel about yourself creates internal and external harmony. However, being perceived as a peacemaker when you feel taken for granted and undermined in the relationship can make you feel resentful of others.

As someone who is codependent, you tend to prioritize your self-image (what others think of you) over your authentic self (what you think about yourself). As a result, you often feel unfulfilled in your relationships because your genuine thoughts, feelings, personality traits, and attitudes are never appreciated and validated. Your friends, relatives, and colleagues validate your self-image, which, for a while, makes you feel good but, in the long run, creates a disconnect. Ironically, there is nothing more that you desire than for people to get to know the real you. Nevertheless, you are afraid they may not be as excited about or accepting of who you are.

This is why you crave external validation. Being well-liked by others substitutes for having to open up and let people truly experience who you are by creating a false sense of security and belonging. Due to the fear of abandonment and other codependency issues that you may have, you unconsciously believe that it is safer to keep people at an emotional distance by introducing them to your self-image instead of your authentic self.

In the end, nobody wins. Your loved ones never get the opportunity to connect with you deeply, and you don't get the opportunity to be vulnerable and seen as the amazing person that you are. The truth is that people-pleasing pleases no one, and therefore, it is a harmful behavior that should be addressed as part of your codependency recovery.

The People-Pleasing Paradox

People-pleasing seeks to make others satisfied and, in doing so, earn their approval, affection, and support. By studying what people need from you and modifying your behavior accordingly, you can almost guarantee a stable relationship. Nevertheless, all of this comes at the cost of expressing your needs and expectations, and therein lies the paradox of people-pleasing. The pursuit of making others satisfied paradoxically causes you to feel unsatisfied because you undermine your needs when you prioritize the needs of others.

Think of moments during childhood when you "performed" for your parents to receive their attention and affection. You learned what behaviors they liked and disliked and started to behave in ways that would win them over. For example, if your parents expected good grades, you worked hard to get straight grades to receive praise from them. The motivation wasn't based on what you desired for yourself but instead on what your parents desired for you. Therefore, to continue to make them happy, you had to play the role of a high-achieving son or daughter.

Performances don't make you feel good about yourself because you are acting. Even if the performance is unconscious (i.e., you are unaware that you are playing a specific role), your habits and routines don't bring fulfillment. On the outside, you could have all of the symbols of success, but internally, you don't feel successful because you are disconnected from the role you are playing. Or maybe you have a relationship that looks strong and healthy on the outside and makes others envious, but internally, you feel lonely and disconnected from your partner or friend.

The reason why people-pleasing doesn't bring long-term happiness is that you are encouraged to be someone you are not. In the process, you neglect your needs and desires and adopt a lifestyle that doesn't bring out the best in you. This explains why people-pleasing can be exhausting and frustrating—you spend a lot of energy constructing a false identity that doesn't feel rewarding. In other words, you don't get pleasure from the investments you make in building relationships with others.

A real-life story that captures this was told by author, businesswoman, and comedian Kathy Klotz-Guest. Many years ago, before she started her marketing business, Kathy worked in the high-tech field. She felt like a fish out of water, being one of a few women working in a fast-paced, male-dominated space. Besides being a woman, what made Kathy stand out like a sore thumb was her bubbly personality. She was told several times by other women that she needed to quit being open and humorous if she wanted to be taken seriously.

Of course, at the time, Kathy desired to advance in her career, so she decided to take this advice and change how she showed up at work. She started to blend in with her colleagues and water down her big personality to make others feel less uncomfortable around her. She received promotions and slowly climbed up the career ladder, as she had planned. However, she became restless and unhappy when she thought about how much of herself she had to hide or downplay in her work environment.

Eventually, she quit her career and turned to entrepreneurship. Being the boss meant that she could create a work culture that embraced what she stood for. She used her humor as an asset to build her business, connect with like-minded people, and come up with innovative marketing ideas. Reflecting on her career journey thus far, Kathy comments:

> I am primarily concerned about acting in accordance with my values, my soul, my creativity, and my sensibilities. Just recently, for example, I walked away from an opportunity because it was not in alignment with what I wanted to do and how I wanted to show up in the world. Saying no according to your values is a muscle. The more you do it, the easier it gets and the better your world gets (Klotz-Guest, 2016).

From External Validation to Internal Validation

Humans are social creatures and depend on each other for survival. You need reassurance and support from others to build a strong sense of self and find your place in the world. Positive interactions with loved ones and colleagues help you construct aspects of your identity because these encounters allow you to reflect on who you are and what you need. Therefore, external validation is not a bad thing. What's bad is relying solely on what others think of you to build your identity.

So, when do things start to go wrong? In many cases, excessive reliance on external validation originates from childhood. Feelings of rejection result from a continuous cycle of hurt and invalidation from your loved ones. You begin to doubt your inherent worth and contributions to the world because the people around you don't respect you. Oftentimes, young children are taught to respect their elders, but they don't deserve respect in return. As a result, they start to perceive other people as being smarter and more capable than them.

You may have battled with a low sense of self-worth if you were disrespected as a child. Examples of disrespectful behaviors are being ignored by your parents, having your ideas dismissed or shut down, being harshly criticized for your personal attributes, or being told that who you are is not good enough. All of these behaviors, and more, cause rejection and invalidation, which encourage seeking external validation.

Excessive external validation shifts your focus to the outside world. All of the answers about who you are, what you need, and what you should strive to achieve are based on the opinions of others. It can be difficult to break this cycle of looking to others for validation because, growing up, you were made to feel insignificant without other people. Nobody encouraged you to explore your beliefs and embrace your emotions. Life was planned out for you, and you were forced to adopt preconceived ideas that were reinforced at home and throughout your culture.

Early childhood experiences of rejection and abandonment can haunt you for a lifetime and constantly make you feel unfulfilled with your life. No matter how hard you work or how much you develop your character, there is still a negative voice in your head that reminds you of your weaknesses or compares you to other people who you perceive as being better than you. To address and overcome your need for approval from others, it is important to start validating yourself through internal validation.

Internal validation refers to evaluating yourself based on personal beliefs, values, and standards. Imagine that you have your own criteria for what an honorable man or woman should be like, and you are constantly measuring yourself based on those standards, not what society and others expect from you. Your principles and the values that are most important to you inform your criteria, which makes them valid. In other words, how you interact with the world and approach relationships is connected to what you care about and what you need on a fundamental level.

Shifting from external to internal validation can be challenging when you don't have a stable sense of self. It is crucial to know what you want and value before you can set personal expectations for yourself. This means that your ability to validate yourself is linked to your level of self-awareness. Awareness of your thoughts, emotions, desires, and motivations makes it easier to focus on yourself rather than turn to others. You learn to trust your instincts and respect your opinions and beliefs, even when others don't agree with you or choose to walk away.

Don't confuse validating yourself with excusing your bad behaviors or defending yourself even when you are wrong. Internal validation is about recognizing your power to make choices concerning your life. You are no longer that shy, guarded, and disempowered boy or girl who didn't have a voice and couldn't freely express themselves. You are the highest authority in your life and can make choices that improve your well-being, which includes choices about the people you associate with, the boundaries you set in relationships, and the standards you set for yourself and others.

Embracing Authenticity Over Approval

An effective way to overcome seeking external validation is to practice showing up as your authentic self. Being authentic means permitting yourself to be who you are without worrying about how you will be perceived. As you can imagine, this requires openness and vulnerability. If you are not used to being open and vulnerable, being authentic can feel awkward. It takes courage to allow yourself to think and feel whatever you want to think and feel.

Note that this may not always be appropriate based on your circumstances. For example, at work, expressing your authentic self is not always acceptable because you are expected to uphold certain professional standards. Similarly, there are times when showing up as your authentic self is not suitable around family because that may cause them to overstep your boundaries.

Since embracing authenticity is difficult and requires practice, consider being authentic with yourself first. Dedicate some months to adjusting the relationship you have with yourself so that you can allow more room for authenticity. During this time, challenge yourself to validate your thoughts, feelings, and motivations. Listen to what you have to say, acknowledge your emotions, explore your beliefs, and make choices that feel good for you. Once again, authenticity may not be suitable in all contexts of your life, so take a moment to reflect on the appropriateness of your decisions before acting on them.

Here are some practical strategies that can help you embrace authenticity:

Define Actions That Are Authentic and Inauthentic

Spend some time thinking about your interactions with others, focusing on specific relationships where your codependency tendencies are apparent. Reflect on common reactions or behaviors that have become second nature in these relationships. Write down a list of these behaviors in your notebook. Remember to reflect on how you show up in these relationships instead of how others might show up. Go through each behavior and determine whether it is authentic or inauthentic, using the following questions as references:

- Is the behavior something that you genuinely desire to do (authentic) or something you feel obligated to do (inauthentic)?
- Is the behavior motivated by love (authentic) or fear (inauthentic)?
- Is the behavior transactional (inauthentic) or done with no strings attached (authentic)?

Define and Live by Your Values

Core values are the principles that make your life feel meaningful. These tend to be broad principles that apply to different aspects of your life, such as collaboration, acceptance, honesty, and discipline. Discovering and defining your core values can help you live a structured life with clear standards and boundaries. Your values determine how you interact with other people, how you approach work, how you spend your time, and the type of goals you strive for.

Living by your values can also make it easier to set personal limits, identify unacceptable behaviors in others, and build the type of relationships you desire.

If you are unclear about your values, go through the table below, identify the values that resonate with you, and write them down in your notebook. Narrow down the list to 10 values and then again to your top five values. Write down statements describing how you can practically live out your top five values daily.

love	adventure	justice	learning
peace	wisdom	authenticity	challenge
acceptance	kindness	friendship	personal growth
spirituality	punctuality	independence	health
honesty	ambition	security	beauty
discipline	creativity	balance	altruism
community	trust	leadership	respect
family	integrity	change	success

Acknowledge Internal and External Influences

Consider who or what informs your decisions or behaviors. For example, do you act based on what you believe is right or what others expect from you? Do you pursue goals that you have always desired or goals that would make you appear desirable to other people?

Internal influences are ideas, beliefs, or values that inform how you think and the actions you take. External influences are societal expectations that you have been conditioned from birth to aim for and achieve. The decisions that you make concerning your life or relationships can be traced back to either internal or external influences. At any given moment, you are behaving based on what you think and feel or what others expect from you.

Your inner voice gives you clues about which type of influence is operating. For example, whenever you hear yourself using the word "should," like "I should call them back," there is an external influence. The tone and language of your inner voice will also indicate who influences your thoughts. For example, hearing your own voice is a sign that you are thinking or making decisions out of your free will. However, hearing someone else's voice (i.e., a critical parent or ex-partner) or a judgmental, critical voice means that some external force (whether real or imagined) is influencing your mind.

It can also be helpful to ask yourself why you think and feel a certain way. For instance, why do you struggle to stand up for yourself? Is it based on an internal or external influence? If based on an internal influence, what belief or assumption causes you to be afraid to stand up for yourself? If based on an external influence, what social expectation could you be operating under? Understanding what influences your thoughts, emotions, and behaviors can encourage you to live more authentically and make choices that align with who you are and what you desire.

Saying no can be painful when you are a people-pleaser. You may fear that setting a boundary will cause other people to feel upset, which could potentially backfire on you. While nobody enjoys hearing the word no, it is important to be clear about what you can and cannot tolerate in relationships. This level of honesty allows others to manage their expectations of you and learn more about how you desire to be treated.

You can build the courage to say no by being attuned to your wants and needs. Whenever someone requests a favor, pay attention to your body. After they have made their request known, what immediate thought comes to your mind? Does your body feel tense or relaxed? Furthermore, consider how much energy or time you have left at your disposal and whether you could comfortably fulfill their request without compromising your well-being. If the answer is not a quick and enthusiastic yes, take it as a no.

There are many ways to say no without coming across as rude while remaining assertive. Find a mirror in your home and practice the following scripts using different tones of voice (e.g. calm, firm, gentle, serious, etc.). These scripts can be used in different contexts and types of relationships. You can also come up with your own scripts that are relevant to your real-life situations.

- Saying no when you don't have time right now: "Thank you for reaching out. I am unavailable at the moment. Can we set a time for next week?"
- Saying no when the plan doesn't work for you: "I love the idea and where we are going with this. Can we brainstorm more suggestions?"
- Saying no and making a referral: "I don't know much about property costs, but my husband does. Would you like to speak with him?"

- Saying no but expressing gratitude: "I appreciate the invitation; however, I won't be available that weekend."
- Saying no partially: "I am willing to help you find a new gym, but you will have to attend classes by yourself."
- Saying no and offering an explanation: "I won't be available for the meeting because I have a lot of work to complete this week."

____

____

____

____

____

____

____

____

Seeking external validation isn't a bad thing; however, it should never become your central focus. Outside of what people think, you have a rich, multi-dimensional identity that cannot be compared to anyone else. You are one-of-a-kind, which means that when people encounter you, they can never share the same experience with anyone else. It is important to focus on building a stable sense of self and creating personal standards by which you live. This will help you manage your expectations, set healthy boundaries with others, and live an authentic existence. The following chapter continues to empower your authentic self by helping you rediscover your voice.

Make a Difference with Your Review: Unlock the Power of Helping Others

In helping others, we shall help ourselves, for whatever good we give out completes the circle and comes back to us. –Flora Edwards

"

Helping others not only feels good but also makes a big difference in the world. That's why I have a special question for you today...

Would you be willing to help someone you've never met, without expecting anything in return?

Imagine someone out there who is just like you used to be—maybe feeling a bit lost, searching for answers, or hoping to break free from the cycle of codependency. They need guidance, just like you once did.

That's where the Codependency Recovery Workbook comes into play. My goal is to get this life-changing book into the hands of as many people as possible because I believe in its power to transform lives. But I can't do this alone.

The truth is, many people rely on reviews when deciding whether to invest in a book. So here's my heartfelt request on behalf of a fellow reader you've never met:

Please consider leaving a review for this book.

Your feedback doesn't cost a dime and takes less than a minute to share, but it could profoundly impact someone else's journey toward healing and growth. Your review could be the nudge that helps someone:

- Start their journey of personal healing.
- Discover tools to build healthier relationships.
- Gain the confidence to set boundaries and reclaim their independence.
- Learn techniques that could change their life's path.
- Embark on a transformative personal journey.

Scan the QR code or click this link to leave your review:

If you feel a spark of joy knowing you could help someone in such a simple yet impactful way, then you're exactly the kind of person I love to connect with. Welcome to the club—you're one of us now!

I'm excited to help you navigate the path to healthier relationships and personal empowerment. You're going to find the strategies and lessons in the upcoming chapters incredibly valuable.

Thank you from the bottom of my heart for your support. Let's return to our journey of growth and learning together.

With gratitude, Lulu Nicholson

P.S. - Remember, when you offer something valuable to someone, you become more valuable in their eyes. If you think this book could help another person like it helped you, consider sharing it with them.

Rediscovering Your Voice—How to Craft Open and Healthy Dialogues With Others

It took me quite a long time to develop a voice, and now that I have it, I am not going to be silent. –Madeleine K. Albright

"

Communication Clashes

Robert and Ursula had been married for three years when they decided to go to couples therapy. Their main issue was the differences in their communication styles. Robert was the type of person who would bottle his feelings and wait until they became overwhelming before he spoke up. He would downplay his concerns and talk himself out of addressing what he didn't like in their relationship. Since he kept his problems to himself, Ursula couldn't tell when she had crossed the line, which meant that she couldn't modify her behaviors and respond to his needs.

Ursula was a different type of communicator. She was overly expressive of her thoughts and emotions and often shared too much information. For example, when she was upset, she would spend hours speaking about her hurt feelings. Her oversharing and accusatory statements like "You did this to me..." made the atmosphere tense at home and caused Robert to become defensive and emotionally shut down. Ursula read Robert's behavior as a sign of rejection, which made her feel even more frustrated and misunderstood.

In couples therapy, the married couple learned how to communicate effectively with each other by practicing a technique known as open communication. Open communication taught the couple how to share their thoughts and feelings without passing blame or judgment on one another. Moreover, instead of communicating on opposite sides of problems, they were shown how to listen and empathize with each others' concerns and collaborate on solving problems together.

Robert walked away from therapy with the confidence to express his thoughts and feelings. However, he needed Ursula to create an emotionally safe space for him to be vulnerable without feeling judged. Ursula also agreed to be mindful of how she communicated information to prevent making Robert feel responsible for her pain. She also expressed how she needs her partner to validate her thoughts and feelings so that she will know without a doubt that he understands where she is coming from. Robert agreed to this and also committed to being more emotionally present during difficult conversations rather than being quick to put up walls.

The Power of Open and Healthy Communication

If relationships were houses, communication would be the pillars that hold the structure together. Think back to the first time you met your partner or best friend. They were a perfect stranger whom you knew little about. Your conversations were light and surface-level because you hadn't yet built a foundation of trust.

However, to build trust, both of you had to willingly engage in many conversations, opening up to one another more each time. Once the foundation of trust had been built, you had to continue communicating openly to establish a strong emotional connection and ensure both of your relationship needs were being fulfilled.

In many relationships, couples, friends, and colleagues fail to keep the lines of communication open long enough to establish a foundation of trust. Others may successfully form trust but fail to sustain healthy relationships with ongoing open dialogue. The truth is that communication should never stop in relationships. When it does, there are usually serious underlying issues at play, such as:

- **Poor listening from one or both parties:** Open communication involves taking turns to listen and speak. The type of listening required is active listening, where the listener blocks out all distractions and pays attention to the verbal and nonverbal cues shared by the speaker to thoroughly understand their message. Failure to practice active listening can lead to conflict and misunderstandings.

- **Unspoken thoughts and feelings:** It is difficult to open up to someone when you feel hidden resentment toward them. Unspoken thoughts and feelings are the messages that you fail to express due to fears like the fear of judgment or the fear of rejection. They can cause you to become defensive, avoidant, or passive-aggressive when communicating with your loved ones.

- **Unrealistic communication expectations:** Sometimes, communication is cut off because of unrealistic rules about what can be communicated and what can't be communicated. For example, there could be certain topics in your relationship that are "off bounds" or certain emotions like anger that are seen as communication red flags and cause you to disengage. These expectations set you up for failure because they create an unnatural dialogue based on fear of not saying the wrong things and upsetting the other person.

- **Different communication styles:** Being compatible with someone doesn't mean that they will share the same communication style as you. For example, you might be a straightforward person who prefers direct communication, while your partner might be more diplomatic and prefer a subdued and understated way of sharing information. The inability to learn and adjust to each other's communication styles can cause unnecessary conflict.

- **Attachment issues:** Your attachment style can influence the way you communicate with others. In most cases, your style of communication will be similar to how you expressed your thoughts and feelings as a child. Unless you identify and address your attachment issues, you may continue to feel misunderstood by your loved one, while failing to empathize with where they are coming from.

Open communication takes commitment from both parties. You need to commit to being honest with each other and sharing how you feel, even when what you have to say isn't pleasant. You need to commit to listening to each other, even when you disagree. Furthermore, you need to commit to respecting each other's viewpoints and empathizing with your unique experiences. Without this level of commitment coming from both of you, expressing your true thoughts and feelings could feel unsafe and, therefore, not something you wish to do.

Rediscovering Your Lost Voice and Speaking With Self-Conviction

If you are struggling with open communication, take a moment to reflect on what specific issues are getting in your way. Acknowledge your own communication fears or habits that could be making it difficult to connect with your loved ones. Additionally, consider how your patterns of codependency have made communicating your true thoughts and feelings tough.

For example, due to the fear of abandonment, you may be afraid of voicing your concerns, disagreeing openly with others, communicating boundaries, or making your needs and requests known. All of these codependency issues have the potential to block open communication in your relationships. Alternatively, they could motivate you to adopt unhealthy communication habits to convey your messages, such as:

- belittling or judging others
- being rigid and refusing to compromise
- being controlling of others
- giving the silent treatment to show disapproval
- denying your part in relationship problems
- becoming defensive when you feel attacked

Healthy communication is not about who's right or wrong but about how two people can openly and respectfully exchange ideas to solve problems and develop a stronger bond. To achieve this, there must be mutual respect and a willingness to listen. Furthermore, boundaries should be put in place to prevent toxic communication patterns. The following is a list of common toxic communication patterns and examples of how to overcome them in your relationships.

Defensiveness

Defensive communication feels like putting up a wall and countering what someone is saying without taking the time to listen and understand where they are coming from. Your immediate response could be to deflect, deny, blame, or downplay what they are saying. Defensiveness stems from deep-rooted insecurities and fears. It may also be a communication pattern that you picked up in childhood, either as a coping mechanism or something you learned from your parents.

Instead of being defensiveness: Listen without creating stories or assumptions in your mind about the meaning behind the message. If you are feeling attacked, consider whether you have mistakenly personalized a message that has nothing to do with you. Remember, when someone shares their thoughts and feelings, they are opening up and allowing you to step into their world. Their strong feelings are not attacks on who you are. Step out of your shoes and empathize with where they are coming from.

Contempt

Contempt is mean-spirited communication that is intended to inflict hurt. It is a passive-aggressive strategy that shows disapproval of how someone else might feel or behave. An example of contempt is eye-rolling, criticism, acting superior, speaking in a mocking tone of voice, or showing expressions of disgust on your face. Behind contempt are a lot of unspoken thoughts and feelings that have caused a buildup of resentment and disrespect.

Instead of showing contempt: Take the risk and be honest about your thoughts and feelings, even if it means upsetting the other person. Honesty creates an opening for vulnerability and meaningful conversations. For example, if you are hurt, be honest and share your hurt feelings. Use the "I feel...I need" statement to share your emotions and make direct requests. You might say, "I feel frustrated when you don't respect my ability to think for myself. I need you to support me by allowing me to make decisions for myself."

Criticism

Criticism involves setting expectations for someone and judging them when they don't live up to those expectations. It can also be seen as a form of projection of things that you struggle to accept or embrace about yourself. For example, you might criticize someone for lying, even though you have a difficult time being truthful about your thoughts and feelings. Criticism might also be used as a passive-aggressive way of getting someone to respond to your needs, especially when you fear being open and direct about them.

Instead of criticism: Whenever you feel the urge to criticize someone, empathize with their life circumstances first. Ask questions and seek to understand before making assumptions about who they are or what they have intended to do. Another way to combat criticism is to think about what you appreciate about the individual and how they have positively impacted your life. This allows you to see both their strengths and weaknesses.

Control

Control involves influencing someone to feel or behave in certain ways. In many cases, particularly with codependent people, controlling behavior is unintentional. For example, due to your fear of abandonment, you may feel anxious when you cannot anticipate someone else's behavior. Safety for you means being able to predict your loved one's behaviors and create a controlled environment in your relationship to avoid common relationship problems.

Instead of control: Combat controlling behavior by finding ways to feel secure in yourself outside of your loved one's actions. For example, strengthening your boundaries, articulating your needs, and standing up for yourself when you feel mistreated are some of the ways to reduce anxiety in relationships. It is also important to surround yourself with positive people whom you trust and can rely on. This can minimize your need for control because their behaviors are respectful and considerate of your needs (i.e., they can make you feel emotionally safe in your relationships).

Misrepresentation

Misrepresentation is the incorrect interpretation of a message that is due to selective listening. Instead of focusing on what is being communicated through verbal or nonverbal language, you might cut corners by oversimplifying, making accusations, or distorting the message. There are many reasons why you might do this. For instance, the message could be something difficult to hear because it goes against what you think or feel. You may also seek to defend yourself by invalidating what the other person is saying.

Instead of misrepresentation: When you are feeling emotional, excuse yourself from a conversation and take a few minutes to calm yourself. Engaging in a discussion when your emotions are high can lead to defensiveness and, subsequently, misrepresentation. Furthermore, approach tough conversations with a willingness to understand where the other person may be coming from. To do this, you must listen carefully, not only to what they are communicating verbally but also to their body language.

Take out your notebook and journal about your experiences speaking with conviction in your relationships. Write a page about your communication struggles and strengths in the four categories of relationships: romantic, family, social, and professional. Identify the toxic communication patterns that exist in these relationships and how they have impacted the way you relate to and connect with others. Lastly, make a note of behaviors you would like to change or modify to improve your quality of communication in all four types of relationships.

EXERCISE

Positive Dialogues Cheat Sheet

It is important to get as much practice communicating openly and honestly with others. To help you get started, here is a list of positive communication phrases that will help you foster healthy dialogue.

Instead of saying this...	**Practice saying this...**
Don't make me angry.	When you [describe upsetting behavior], I feel angry. Please stop doing that.
Just leave me alone.	I feel overwhelmed right now. Could you please give me five minutes to cool down?
I'm fine.	I'm not okay with that, but I still need time to process my feelings. I'll come to you when I'm ready to talk.
Why do you act like that?	I noticed you tend to [describe peculiar behavior]. I'm curious to know why you do that.
I'm done with this conversation.	I don't think this conversation is constructive. Could we please take a break or postpone it to another time?
You don't listen to me.	I get angry when you misinterpret what I'm saying. Are you listening to me?
You need my help.	I care for you and want to help you. Are you open to receiving my help?
I give up. There's no point talking to you.	It seems to me like you are not willing to hear me out. Could you kindly excuse me from this conversation?
[Insert name] does it better than you.	I respect your process, even though I have seen it done another way. Keep going, and let me know if you need help.
It was just a joke. Relax.	I realize that my statement was hurtful. It was not my intention to offend you. I am sorry.

Stop being so sensitive.	I can tell that this matter makes you emotional. Would you like to share more about how you feel?
I don't care.	I am hurt by what you have said and wish we could have an open conversation to resolve our differences.
I'm disappointed in you.	I feel upset because I expected more from you.
I hate that about you.	I dislike it when you [describe upsetting behavior]. It makes me feel [name the emotion].
Why are you so triggered?	You look visibly upset, and I think we should take a break from the conversation.
[silent treatment]	I am hurt but don't have the words to fully express how I feel. Can you give me some time alone?
[mocking laughter]	I disagree with what you have to say, but I still respect your opinion.
[eye rolling]	I don't quite understand where you are coming from. Could you please explain what you mean by [describe what you don't understand]?

Open communication enables you to share your honest thoughts and emotions without feeling judged. To practice this type of communication in your relationships, full commitment is required by both parties. This is because open communication is about taking turns speaking and listening, validating and being validated. Therefore, both people should exhibit qualities like openness, patience, and empathy. Closely tied to open communication, the next chapter teaches you how to communicate and enforce healthy boundaries.

The Limits of Yes and No—How to Set Strong Boundaries

When we fail to set boundaries and hold people accountable, we feel used and mistreated. This is why we sometimes attack who they are, which is far more hurtful than addressing a behavior or a choice.
–Brené Brown

“

The Difficulty of Setting Boundaries

Imagine building your dream home and spending hundreds of thousands of dollars furnishing each room but not fitting any doors or windows. Your home could be worth millions, but the lack of security measures increases the risk of potential robberies and unwanted visitors coming in and out of your home. You are an expensive home worth millions, and your boundaries are the doors, windows, alarm systems, and fences you set up to protect your well-being. Without boundaries, you are vulnerable to being mistreated and finding yourself in unhealthy relationships.

Boundaries are not synonymous with punishing others, even though this could be what you were taught growing up. For example, if you have an anxious, avoidant, or disorganized attachment to your parents, you may have been raised in a household where children were not allowed to say no to their parents, express their limits, refuse requests, or stand up for themselves when they felt bullied. Your parents set the rules, and you were instructed to follow them without questioning their appropriateness. You may have also been punished for sharing ideas or opinions that went against family norms. This is common for children who are labeled as the “black sheep” of their families.

Due to your lack of education about boundaries as a child, you may be afraid of setting limits with others. Having boundaries could seem like a disadvantage to making friends and gaining approval from others. Because you don't want them to feel rejected, you avoid saying no to people. Subconsciously, the feeling of rejection is how you felt when your parents disregarded your needs and requests. For as long as setting boundaries is synonymous with pain and punishment, you won't feel motivated to put up these fences and protect your interests. It is, therefore, necessary to redefine what boundaries mean to you and see the value of prioritizing your needs.

What, Exactly, Are Personal Boundaries?

Almost all relationship therapists will tell you that to improve the quality of your relationships, you must establish and communicate boundaries. Personal boundaries are the invisible limits that separate your interests from other people's interests. They are the building blocks of trust, respect, and emotional safety in relationships. Having personal boundaries is not about shutting people out. Instead, it is about communicating your likes and dislikes so that people know how to relate to you.

Despite how compatible you are with your partner, friends, colleagues, or family members, the fact remains that you are different people. What you need and expect from your relationships won't be the same. What makes you different from each other are the unique life experiences you have been through that have informed how you connect with people and what you look for in relationships. Personal boundaries seek to communicate those differences by teaching each other what acceptable and unacceptable behavior looks like.

There is no other way for people to know what you need or expect from them if you don't communicate your boundaries. And yes, sometimes communicating boundaries is uncomfortable because you don't want to hurt other people's feelings. However, consider the consequences of allowing them to continue behaving in ways that you deem unacceptable. How much more pain and problems would be created by keeping quiet? The truth is, there is only so much mistreatment you can take before you retaliate through aggressive or passive-aggressive behaviors. The silent treatment is a good example of what happens when boundaries are not communicated clearly and enforced with proper consequences.

Even if people don't approve of your boundaries, they are likely to respect them because they are invested in your relationship and want to create a harmonious environment for both of you. Likewise, you won't always agree with others' boundaries, but because you care about your relationship and know how much certain things mean to them, you are likely to adjust your expectations and respect their wishes. People who refuse to respect your boundaries simply aren't invested in the relationship enough to make it work. They may care for you but are not prepared to learn about who you are and what you need to feel safe, loved, and respected.

With that said, there are times when people will ask you to adjust your boundaries or compromise to accommodate their needs and expectations. Remember, relationships are built by two unique individuals with diverse life experiences. Thus, it is normal to experience a clash of interests even when you are compatible with each other. However, it is important to evaluate which of your boundaries are negotiable and which ones are non-negotiable. Once again, this should be communicated upfront with others so that they know when to challenge your boundaries and when they cannot.

For example, in romantic relationships, there is a general expectation for couples to text or call each other daily. For you, daily communication with your partner may not be a big deal. Perhaps you are comfortable skipping days without reaching out to your partner, which makes this expectation negotiable (i.e., it isn't classified as a dealbreaker). However, your partner needs daily, engaging communication to stay connected to you. Perhaps quality time is one of their love languages, and when they cannot physically be with you, they want to be able to reach you on the phone. The lack of daily communication could be a non-negotiable boundary for them, which means that it isn't something they are willing to compromise.

This ultimately means that you are required to adjust your expectations to make your partner feel secure in the relationship. Later down the line, there will be boundaries that are non-negotiables for you, and your partner will have to adjust their expectations to make you feel secure in the relationship. If there is ever a time when both of you have non-negotiable positions on an issue, this is when both sides must compromise. This give-and-take continues over and over again until you create an ideal culture in your relationship.

Different Types of Healthy Boundaries

The purpose of setting boundaries is to make you feel secure in your relationships. Therefore, you cannot set only one boundary; you need to have a few to cover different kinds of situations that make you feel uncomfortable. The more boundaries you set and communicate, the easier it becomes for others to understand you as an individual and how you desire to be treated.

Below are some examples of healthy boundaries you can establish in your relationships:

Physical Boundaries

Physical boundaries are about proximity to others. They deal with situations involving physical distance, personal space, and physical touch. For example, in the office, you prefer colleagues to stand an arm's length away from you. At home, you prefer guests staying within a certain area and not going into other rooms. With friends, you prefer handshakes or high-fives instead of hugs.

Sexual Boundaries

Sexual boundaries apply to romantic relationships only. They are based on your sexual preferences and expectations. Since intimacy is such a big component of healthy romantic relationships, it is crucial to define what it looks like for you. If there are sexual behaviors that you aren't willing to try or specific rules that need to be observed (e.g., asking for consent, waiting a specific period to have sex, etc.), it is important to communicate these before engaging in sexual experiences.

Emotional Boundaries

Emotional boundaries protect your feelings from being exploited in relationships. For example, they seek to protect you from being disrespected, invalidated, emotionally abused, or having your needs dismissed. These boundaries also communicate to others how you desire to be spoken to, comforted, and shown affection through your love languages.

Material Boundaries

Material boundaries set limits and expectations about how much access others have to your material possessions, such as your home, vehicles, money, clothing, and so on. They draw the line between being generous and being taken for granted or exploited. Material boundaries can change over time. For example, when you were single, you were comfortable having your friends come to your house every weekend, but now that you are in a relationship, you want to restrict them to once or twice a month.

Time Boundaries

Time boundaries control how much attention you give to different people or tasks, or which people or tasks take priority in your life. These types of boundaries are particularly important in the workspace to manage coworkers' expectations of you. Nevertheless, they apply to other aspects of your life, too, such as honoring or declining invitations, scheduling important conversations or family meetings, or allocating time to practicing self-care.

Setting Boundaries in Easy and Difficult Situations

Setting boundaries is like preparing a dish. If you add the incorrect ingredients, follow the wrong instructions, or get the timing off, you will end up with something you never expected. Thus, it is important to follow the correct methods when setting boundaries to ensure that your message is received in the best way possible.

Some people will honor your boundaries without hesitation, and others will find it difficult to accept them. When approaching boundary conversations, remember to manage your expectations, instead of going in with the desire to receive an enthusiastic response to your boundaries, leave room for disappointment. Prepare yourself for both easy and difficult situations.

You cannot guarantee positive outcomes all of the time, but there are ways to improve your delivery and communicate in a manner that causes the other person to understand and respect your boundaries. Some of the tips to remember include:

1. **State your needs without telling people what they should do.**

Clearly describe what you need or what your concerns are without telling the other person how they should act. The fact is, you cannot motivate someone to change, especially when they continue to violate your boundaries. Your job is to make sure they understand where you are coming from and allow them to modify their behaviors on their own.

2. **Get the timing right.**

Before communicating your boundaries, make sure the other person is in the right frame of mind and has enough time and energy to listen to what you have to say. Stressful periods of the day or month are not the best time to bring up boundary conversations. Ensure that you are both calm and emotionally regulated and don't have too much going on in your lives.

3. **Be direct and avoid overexplaining.**

Your boundaries are rules or limits that you are certain about. You have spent time thinking about what you want from the relationship and why these things matter to you. Therefore, when communicating your boundaries, be direct about what you need. This shows how much confidence you have in yourself and the importance of the request you are making. Avoid vague or long explanations that could come across, such as trying to convince the other person to support your request.

4. **Keep the focus on you.**

Don't fall into the trap of thinking that your boundaries are universal. Not everybody will agree with or support your boundaries. Moreover, not everybody places the same importance on the things that matter to you. When communicating your boundaries, emphasize your thoughts, feelings, and needs. Use "I believe," "I need," and "I feel" statements to make it clear that your boundaries are what's best for you.

5. Be mindful of your tone and choice of words.

How you communicate your boundaries matters because sometimes people respond defensively due to your strong language or harsh tone of voice. Remember that when you are setting boundaries, you are not making demands. You are simply helping the other person understand what you need from the relationship. Boundary conversations should be non-combative and respectful to allow for open communication and empathy.

6. Accept the reality of your situation.

There are certain things in your relationship that cannot be changed by setting boundaries. Some of these include the other person's character, mindset, beliefs, and values. In most cases, boundaries help to modify harmful habits and attitudes, but they cannot rehabilitate a toxic individual or toxic relationship. Therefore, if you find yourself in dysfunctional relationships, it is best to leave those relationships or accept that certain critical aspects of your relationships cannot be fixed.

7. Don't ask for something they cannot give you.

When setting boundaries, consider who you are making your requests to and manage your expectations accordingly. This goes back to accepting the reality of your situation. For example, some people in your life cannot respond to your emotional needs because of their psychological issues. Continuing to ask them to behave in ways they cannot will create conflict in your relationships. It is better to expect less from them and enforce appropriate physical boundaries to prevent them from repeatedly hurting or disrespecting you.

Creating and Maintaining Strong, Wise, and Healthy Boundaries

The tips above are useful when you are preparing to set boundaries. However, the actual process of deciding what you are going to say requires a different strategy. Below are five detailed steps on how you can formulate strong, wise, and healthy boundaries and present them appropriately.

Step 1: Reflect on What You Want From the Relationship

In every relationship, you will have a different set of needs and expectations. For example, at work, punctuality, confidentiality, and respectful communication could be high on your list. In your romantic relationship, physical intimacy, emotional support, and spending time with your partner could describe what you need. Treat each relationship like it is one of its kind and reflect on what would make you feel secure and fulfilled in the relationship.

Step 2: Connect With How You Feel

Tracking your emotions can be a great way to identify the need for boundaries. For example, when you initially get into a romantic relationship, you may feel satisfied with how your partner is treating you. However, as time goes on, you notice that you are less excited about seeing them. By tracking your emotions, you may find that the reason why you are not enthusiastic about seeing your partner is that you are always together (if you are someone who values solitude) or that you haven't found ways of having fun together. Another way to track how you feel is by asking yourself the following questions:

- Did the other person make an unkind joke or comment at your expense?
- Did the other person act in ways that made you feel physically uncomfortable?
- Did the other person's actions make you feel pressured to go against your values?

- Did the way the other person spoke to you make you feel disrespected?
- Did you feel resistant or overwhelmed by the other person's requests or expectations of you?
- Did you feel like the other person was infringing on your rights or sense of control?

Step 3: Visualizing and Defining Your Limits

Now that you have had some time to reflect on your needs or concerns, focus on visualizing and defining your limits. Be very clear and direct about where you draw the line. Imagine that you were tasked with explaining your limits to a five-year-old child. In other words, use simple and relatable language and cut straight to the chase. Defining your limits can be as simple as saying, "I don't like..." followed by the behavior that you deem unacceptable. Here are some examples:

- I don't like it when you talk over me.
- I don't like the tone of voice you are using.
- I don't like it when you criticize my decisions.
- I don't like it when you talk to your family about our problems
- I don't like being gossiped about in the office.

You have the option of following up on how the behavior mentioned makes you feel so that the other person understands why that type of behavior upsets you. Remember to take ownership of your emotions when expressing them to avoid coming across as accusatory. Here are some examples:

- I don't like it when you talk over me. It makes me feel insignificant.
- I don't like the tone of voice you are using. It feels disrespectful to me.
- I don't like it when you criticize my decisions. I feel you don't trust me.

- I don't like it when you talk to your family about our problems. I feel exposed.
- I don't like being gossiped about in the office. It infuriates me.

Step 4: Specify What You Need

Setting limits is important, but they should be followed by specific actions the other person can take to ensure they don't violate your boundaries. Don't assume that they understand what you need. Clearly state what acceptable behavior looks like so they can modify their behaviors with ease. When specifying your needs, be mindful of the other person's boundaries too. For example, don't ask for something that might go against their values or beliefs. Here are some examples:

- I don't like it when you talk over me. It makes me feel insignificant. Please wait until I complete my train of thought before sharing your ideas.
- I don't like the tone of voice you are using. It feels disrespectful to me. Please use a gentle, lowered voice when expressing your thoughts and feelings.
- I don't like it when you criticize my decisions. I feel you don't trust me. Please show support and offer encouraging words when I'm opening up about my plans.
- I don't like it when you talk to your family about our problems. I feel exposed. Please protect the safe place we have created by keeping our relationship matters private.
- I don't like being gossiped about in the office. It infuriates me. Please keep your personal feelings about me to yourself and maintain professionalism.

Step 5: State the Consequences

Healthy boundaries come with consequences to ensure that boundary violations are few and far between. Some difficult people may need consequences to take your boundaries seriously. Moreover, consequences are a way of holding yourself accountable to the standards you desire in your relationships. In other words, if people treat you poorly, you are quick to correct them because there are certain things you need in relationships to feel safe and respected.

You can state consequences by using the 'If...then..." statement. For example, "If you continue to criticize my decisions, then I will no longer share my plans with you." Consequences are not supposed to be used as threats but rather as insight into what will happen if the mistreatment continues. It is, therefore, important to follow through with the consequences when your boundaries are violated. Something else to note is that consequences are not supposed to be harsh punishment that ruins your relationships. They are simply meant to discourage bad behavior by removing the incentive to behave that way.

Timing is also worth considering when stating consequences. For example, for first-time offenders, you don't need to state a consequence because you can assume they didn't know they were violating your boundaries. Therefore, you would simply set a limit and describe how the behavior makes you feel. Consequences are usually appropriate for second-time offenders who have already been given limits and haven't adhered to them. The consequence is communicated to caution them of the possible outcomes of their behaviors. If they continue to violate your boundary after being warned of the consequences (e.g., third-time offenders), the final step is to take action and remain silent. Don't restate the consequences for the second time; simply act on what you said you were going to do.

EXERCISE

These Are My Boundaries

Read over the types of boundaries and five steps to set boundaries sections of this chapter and create personal boundaries and consequences to implement them. For example, when others don't communicate with you respectfully (an emotional boundary), you might disengage from the conversation as a consequence. If you are still not sure about what type of boundaries to set, go over steps 1–3 of setting boundaries. You can also use the five types of boundaries as inspiration to think of healthy limits to enforce in your relationships.

Categories	Personal boundaries	Consequences
Physical boundaries		
Sexual boundaries		
Emotional boundaries		
Material boundaries		
Time boundaries		

Creating and communicating boundaries is crucial for building healthy relationships where both parties feel safe, respected, and accepted for who they are. It is normal to be afraid or feel guilty about drawing boundaries; however, when these feelings occur, remind yourself that your needs and well-being are important to the survival of the relationship. Feeling safe around others encourages you to be authentic and have more value to add. The following chapter shares more about the significance of and how to build and maintain healthy relationships.

A Healthy Two-Way Street—How to Build Healthy Relationships and Maintain Them

Take advantage of the time that people give you, without taking advantage of the people giving you time. –Curtis Tyrone Jones

“

Being of Service to Others

You have often heard the saying, “Relationships are a two-way street.” In simple language, this means that relationships are built on reciprocity—taking turns serving and showing up for each other. Unless you commit to being of service to others and form relationships with people who are willing to be of service to you, your relationships won’t feel satisfactory.

When you are about to cross a two-lane street, you watch for cars coming from the left and right before walking ahead. This is done to avoid prioritizing one lane over the other, which would cause an accident. The best time to cross the street is when the coast is clear, and there are no incoming vehicles on both lanes. Healthy relationships function on a similar concept. One person’s needs cannot take priority over another person’s needs, regardless of the power, resources, or responsibilities they may have.

For example, good employers care about and serve their employees even though they hold a higher position at work and are in charge of more important tasks. Their seniority in the company doesn’t make their needs more urgent or valid than those of their employees. The same goes for romantic relationships, friendships, and family bonds.

Each person might play a different role, but that doesn't make their needs more or less important in their respective relationships.

If we could summarize the purpose of healthy relationships, it would be to build and maintain intimacy. What makes us excited about getting into and staying in relationships is the opportunity to connect with and develop emotional closeness with others. In a workplace setting, intimacy may not be the goal; however, professionals still desire to be understood, feel safe, and earn the respect of their peers. In other words, they want to form professional connections that make them feel good about their jobs or the companies they work for.

One person cannot create true, long-lasting intimacy. This is because the building blocks of intimacy are trust, commitment, communication, mutuality, compassion, and interdependence. These qualities are built on the efforts and energies of two people who are open and curious about understanding and connecting. Oftentimes, long-term relationships struggle to maintain intimacy because, at some point or another, one person emotionally checks out, which means they cannot play their part in nurturing intimacy.

Unmet needs, unresolved trauma, and challenging life transitions that cause two people to drift apart could also be the cause of ongoing conflict and misunderstandings that result in a lack of intimacy. When these conflicts and misunderstandings occur, the challenge becomes finding ways of renegotiating needs, values, beliefs, and boundaries to ensure that the culture of the relationship matches the pace at which both individuals are evolving and becoming better versions of themselves.

The Foundations of a Healthy Relationship

Not all relationships are built with the same materials. What you offer in one type of relationship may not be appropriate or important in another. It is important to have the right mindset and attitude when entering each of the four types of relationships to build the correct materials. Here is a breakdown of the fundamental qualities that are important for romantic, family, social, and professional relationships. Please note that there are some qualities like trust, respect, commitment, and communication that apply to all relationships but may be expressed differently.

Family Relationships

You don't have to choose your family, but you can choose the type of relationship you have with them. Here are some of the fundamental qualities needed to build strong and meaningful relationships with your family members:

- **Respect:** Personal space and privacy are important boundaries to uphold in families to make everyone feel respected. Respect can also be shown by creating and upholding family rules and values and allowing everyone the freedom to share their thoughts and feelings without fear of punishment.

- **Communication:** Conflicts and misunderstandings are common when two or more people are gathered. Thus, the ability to communicate openly and honestly can assist family members in identifying and solving problems together. Everyone's voice, from the youngest to the oldest family member, should be treated with respect and validated.

- **Teamwork:** Families that are united by a vision, set of values, or purpose tend to maintain closeness even when there is conflict. Moreover, they focus on problems rather than pointing fingers at each other. By working as a team, families can leverage the minds, strengths, and talents of every member to execute goals and improve their living environment.

- **Shared values:** To overcome inherent differences, families identify and hold each other accountable to shared values. These are principles that create a sense of direction that the whole family can follow. Family members' values influence how they interact with one another and the general public.

Romantic Relationships

Romantic relationships are different from family relationships because you have a choice about the partner (or partners) you date or marry. There is also a lot more freedom and flexibility to create the ideal intimate relationship that caters to your needs. Here are some fundamental qualities that are common in healthy romantic relationships:

- **Boundaries:** To ensure there is a balance of give-and-take in your relationship or that you don't neglect your needs or go against your values, boundaries are necessary. Note that boundaries can change as the relationship matures, and this is perfectly normal. You simply need to communicate your updated needs and expectations so that your partner knows how and when to modify their behaviors.

- **Empathy:** There are going to be clashes of interests, beliefs, and expectations because of the differences between you and your partner. Showing empathy encourages both of you to speak openly without fear about what you think and feel and have meaningful conversations. Empathy allows you to work out your differences in a way that brings you closer and helps you understand each other better.

- **Sexual intimacy:** Sex is a powerful way to bond with your partner and express your affection through touch. It is an essential part of keeping the chemistry, passion, and emotional connection alive and healthy. Boundaries and conversations around sex are important to have continuously to ensure that you feel safe to explore your bodies and fulfill each other's need for physical closeness.

- **Gratitude:** It is expected for couples to take care of each other; however, showing gratitude for what your partner does for you can make their acts of service feel less like a job and more like an honorable duty. Saying thank you and expressing what you enjoy, feel proud of, or makes you happy creates an incentive for your partner to willingly cater to your needs.

Social Relationships

Social relationships are necessary to fulfill your need for a sense of belonging. Your friendships challenge you, help you grow, and offer support and encouragement during tough times. Here are the fundamental qualities that create healthy friendships:

- **Commitment:** Without making an effort to see your friends, learn more about them, and stay updated on the developments in their lives, the relationships will naturally fizzle out. Because only one person is responsible for maintaining these friendships, rather than both parties, it takes a lot of work to keep them going.

- **Support:** Friendships are built on the ability to access support. Support may come in different forms, depending on the interests that bring you together. Examples of support include emotional support, informational support, career support, and tangible/service-oriented support.

- **Patience:** It is important to ensure a balance of give-and-take in friendships, too. For example, there will be times when you are playing more of a supportive role when helping your friends resolve problems. Showing up for them requires patience because your needs are temporarily put aside. As long as your friendships are reciprocal, being patient and understanding will not cause you to be taken for granted.

- **Forgiveness:** You won't always say the right things or treat your friends kindly, and neither will they say or act properly all of the time. Being able to forgive quickly and move on can strengthen your friendships and help you learn from your mistakes. Again, it cannot be one-sided because the desire to maintain your friendships drives forgiveness.

Professional Relationships

It is unrealistic to expect to have close bonds with all of your colleagues. If you are lucky, you will make a few friends at work, but this shouldn't be your aim. In a professional environment like the workplace, the goal is to build healthy relationships that allow you to collaborate on shared tasks and goals and achieve company objectives. Here are the fundamental qualities that are required:

- **Respect:** To navigate work challenges and diverse opinions and expectations, respect for your coworkers is crucial. Being respectful at work is about being assertive yet considerate of others' feelings when communicating with them or mindful of others' time when making requests or setting up meetings.

- **Communication:** Open communication allows you to not only share your thoughts and feelings with your coworkers, but also listen and seek to understand their perspectives. Being open and honest with each other can also help reduce conflict and misunderstandings that tend to cause office politics.

- **Inclusion:** Your team may consist of people who come from different social and cultural backgrounds. Inclusion enables you to embrace your age, gender, race, religion, or ethnic differences and see them as a strength rather than a barrier to achieving work goals.

- **Compromise:** There could be many amazing ideas and initiatives put on the table at work, but not all of them can be considered. You won't always get your way when it comes to making decisions, not because your strategies are not good but because of the number of interests, voices, and perspectives that need to be considered. Thus, being able to compromise and remain flexible will ensure you can adapt to what's best for your team or organization instead of what's in your best interests.

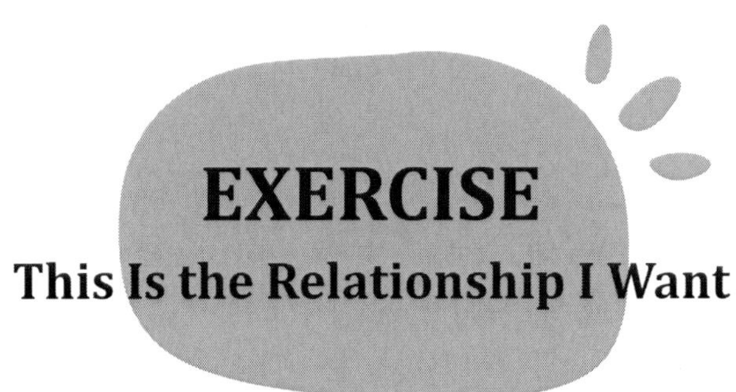

EXERCISE

This Is the Relationship I Want

Many times, we focus on the red flags to watch out for in relationships and overlook the green flags—the qualities and behaviors we desire and look for in others. The purpose of this exercise is to help you reflect on the green flags in the four categories of relationships in your life. This is your time to dream big and visualize your ideal partner, friend, relative, or colleague. Focus on the quality of lifestyle you want to create for yourself and the values that you live by.

Complete the table by responding to the prompts for all four relationship categories.

Categories	I desire someone who is...	So I can fulfill my need for...	And feel...
Family			
Romantic			
Social			
Professional			

Building a Healthier Language of Love

Showing commitment, building trust, and communicating effectively will maintain a healthy relationship, but it doesn't guarantee intimacy. It is possible to respect and care for someone without necessarily feeling a strong emotional connection to them. What strengthens the bond between two people is their ability to speak each other's love languages.

The concept of love languages was developed by Dr. Gary Chapman, who is a marriage counselor. He believed that there were five natural ways in which individuals preferred to receive and express their love for others (Santos-Longhurst, 2022). In most relationships, love languages are not explored or communicated. Each person decides for themselves how they want to express love to their significant other without finding out if that is truly how the recipient desires to be shown love.

This can explain why many long-term romantic relationships experience intimacy issues. Couples become so fixated on loving their partners in their own style that they overlook what their partners need from them. Sometimes, when love languages are communicated, the conversation can lead to conflict, blame, and misunderstandings due to the listener feeling attacked for not responding to their partner's needs in the expected manner.

How someone desires to be loved is considered a non-negotiable boundary because their understanding and experience of love are personal and rooted in their history, personality, values, and belief systems. For example, when you express to your partner that you feel loved when they offer you physical and emotional security, they cannot dispute that or attempt to convince you otherwise. Similarly, when your partner expresses to you that they feel loved when you show physical affection, you cannot debate the pros and cons of showing up for them in that manner.

Part of the reason why, as a codependent person, you have such a difficult time expressing your love needs is because, at some stage in your life, you were made to feel wrong for doing so. As a result, you taught yourself to be satisfied with whatever handouts you received from others rather than specifying what they needed to do to make you feel loved. If you have been in relationships with narcissists (e.g., narcissistic parents or ex-lovers), you may have been made to feel bad or difficult for communicating your needs, which caused you to feel ashamed for desiring the type of love that you do.

Communicating your love languages will feel uncomfortable at first. However, it is an important step to take to ensure that you maintain open and transparent communication with your loved one and prevent repeat cycles of emotional abuse and being stuck in unfulfilling relationships. Please note that if you are still in a romantic relationship with a narcissist, they are incapable of respecting and honoring your needs. Therefore, communicating your love languages to them won't bring the results you hope for.

If you are in a healthy romantic relationship with someone who desires to please you just as much as you desire to please them, then having a conversation about your love languages will feel safe and liberating. Here is a breakdown of the five love languages and how they look from the giver's and receiver's perspectives. Note that love languages do not apply to only romantic relationships; however, in this particular section, we will only focus on how they are displayed in romantic relationships.

Words of Affirmation

Words of affirmation refer to spoken declarations of love, reassurance, support, and encouragement. It involves verbally telling your partner what you think and feel about them. How you share these thoughts and feelings doesn't need to be complicated. For instance, you might express your love through gratitude texts, looking into your partner's eyes and reassuring them that you love them, or giving them handwritten notes and letters mentioning something that you love about them.

Words of affirmation are one of your love languages if you:

- feel good whenever you receive calls and texts from your loved one.
- feel appreciated when your partner shows gratitude.
- expect to be told and affirmed that you are loved often.
- feel happy when your loved one encourages you.

If words of affirmation are one of your partner's love languages, they may expect:

- for you to check in on them throughout the day.
- for you to open up to them about your thoughts and feelings
- for you to be honest and intentional about what you say because words matter to them.

Quality Time

Quality time refers to intentional moments spent with your loved one, usually just the two of you. This doesn't have to be an everyday occurrence (quality, not quantity). However, when you are together, your phones are put away, and the focus is on bonding and enjoying each other's presence. Quality time makes your loved one feel cherished because they have your undivided attention and don't have to compete with other things that you have going on in your life.

Quality time is one of your love languages if you:

- feel lost and disconnected when you cannot reach or be close to your loved one.
- feel upset whenever your loved one is distracted by something or someone else when you are with them.
- feel happy when your loved one makes plans to spend time with you.
- expect to see your loved one or call them frequently during the week.

If quality time is one of your partner's love languages, they may expect:

- to be included in your daily routine.
- to have private moments with you without anybody interrupting.
- less phone use when you are with them.
- being intentional about going out and doing things together.

Physical Touch

Physical touch refers to expressing affection through physical intimacy. The term "physical intimacy" is broad and can include a range of physical acts like holding hands, kissing, cuddling, having sex, sitting close to one another, body strokes, massages, and so on. Physical touch only feels good and affirming if it is consensual, meaning that both you and your partner agree to engage with each other in certain physical ways. For example, if your partner feels loved when you hold their hand in public, but for you, hand-holding feels uncomfortable, doing it just to please them is nonconsensual and won't make them feel loved. Therefore, only physical touch that feels good and is acceptable for both of you will increase intimacy.

Physical touch is one of your love languages if you:

- feel lonely or rejected when you are not held by your loved one.
- feel loved when you receive unexpected kisses and touches.
- enjoy appropriate physical displays of affection in public.

If physical touch is one of your partner's love languages, they may expect:

- to be kissed regularly throughout the day, especially when greeting and departing.
- to be shown appropriate affection in public.
- to prioritize sex in your relationship, even if you need to schedule it.
- to be comforted with touch, such as stroking their back.

Acts of Service

Acts of service refer to selfless tasks that are done to show how much you care about your loved one. It is important to emphasize "selfless" because these tasks may not be important to you. For example, your partner may feel loved when you prepare meals for them, wash the car, pay the bills, pick up their dry-cleaning, and so on. These are chores that they could do for themselves; however, they feel catered to when they are done by someone whom they love.

Acts of service are one of your love languages if you:

- feel loved when your partner does chores without having to be asked.
- desire to feel calm and relaxed in your partner's presence because they have taken care of things.
- feel happy when your partner makes thoughtful gestures like making you coffee in the morning.

If acts of service are one of your partner's love languages, they may expect you to:

- assist them in taking care of their basic needs (e.g., make sure they have eaten).
- book appointments for them to manage their health and their social calendar.
- pick up their favorite snacks and supplies from the store without you being asked.
- identify something they may be struggling with and be proactive in offering solutions.

Receiving Gifts

Receiving gifts refers to tokens of affection that make your partner feel special and loved. It isn't the size of the gift that counts but the thought behind it. By giving your loved one a gift, you communicate how much you care about them and how much you listen to them. The gifts symbolize your love for them and express what cannot be put into words.

Receiving gifts is one of your love languages if you:

- appreciate the thought and level of attention that went into the gifts.
- feel loved when your partner provides material comforts for you.

- feel hurt when your partner doesn't commemorate special occasions without a gift.

If receiving gifts is one of your partner's love languages, they may expect you to:

- take them out to new restaurants or social events.
- pick up their favorite foods or supplies on your way home.
- surprise them with gifts without you being asked.
- buy gifts that are meaningful for your relationship.

It is perfectly normal to have multiple love languages that speak to how you desire to be shown affection. What's important is providing examples of how your partner can practice your love languages. Use positive reinforcement to encourage them to continue practicing their love languages. For example, if you enjoy being held a certain way, let your partner know and make a point of showing appreciation when they do.

An End to the Cycle

Two things to note as you bring the codependency cycle to an end have to do with trust and kindness. As a recovering codependent, you have been hurt by people to whom you gave your loyalty and would do anything. Trusting others isn't something that you do easily because you have been taken advantage of in the past. Nevertheless, trust is required to build healthy relationships. This means that you will need to reach a place where you can lower your guard and be vulnerable again.

With that said, the lessons learned from past experiences have taught you that not everybody can be trusted. Therefore, as you begin to cultivate the relationships you desire, open up slowly and base your level of trust on others' actions rather than how you feel about them; look for physical evidence of their words matching their behaviors, of their commitment to building the relationship, of their ability to reciprocate, and of their willingness to also open up to you and be vulnerable.

Secondly, about kindness, it is important to remember that showing kindness to others isn't a weakness. Only abusive or emotionally unavailable people reject or manipulate your kindness. Generally, people with good intentions will appreciate the love, support, and caregiving you provide and won't make you feel bad for doing so. Nevertheless, being kind should never be used as a tactic to "win over" people. When it is used in this manner, the kindness you show becomes inauthentic and manipulative.

Similar to trust, base the level of kindness and caregiving you provide on the other person's actions. Consider when it is appropriate and inappropriate to show kindness. For example, when somebody doesn't text you back for days on end, being excited and warm toward them when they eventually get back to you is unnatural. You don't necessarily have to be mean when you feel disrespected by someone; however, your actions should show your disapproval of their behavior. Another example is when you see a loved one engaging in a destructive habit. Being kind to them just because you don't want to hurt their feelings is a form of enabling. What they need from you is tough love to know that how they are behind isn't acceptable.

In summary, trust and kindness are both essential qualities in healthy relationships. Therefore, don't stop trusting others or showing kindness. The only thing to be mindful of is who you are trusting and showing kindness to. Opening yourself up and being vulnerable to people who are not kind or trustworthy will only hurt you in the end. It is better to display these wonderful qualities in safe, loving, and supportive relationships where you won't regret it later.

The following chapter shifts the focus back on you and discusses the necessity of self-love in becoming whole and completing yourself.

Only You Can Complete You—How to Master the Art of Unconditional Self-Love

Happiness is an inside job. Don't assign anyone else that much power over your life. –Mandy Hale

"

Being Enough for Yourself

We have spoken about the various causes of codependency, such as childhood trauma, attachment issues, and the fear of abandonment. However, what we haven't yet explored is the belief of not being good enough, which haunts every person with codependency and needs to be addressed and overcome for the cycle to end.

The belief that you are not good enough motivates your codependent behaviors and causes you to put other people at the center of your human existence. Everything you do, whether it is loving your spouse, taking care of your children, starting a business, or living a particular lifestyle, is done because, deep down inside, you have a longing to prove that you are indeed enough and deserving of what you have.

Remember that this isn't something you are always aware of. For example, you are not always aware that your "romantic type" is based on your need to prove something to your peers or that your motivation for accumulating materialistic possessions or living a particular lifestyle is because you feel pressure to silence your self-doubts and self-judgment. However, you will notice when your intentions for pursuing these relationships or symbols of success are not authentic by paying attention to how you feel when you are working toward them or have obtained them. Do you feel satisfied? Are you at peace?

Tracing the origin of this belief will take you back to childhood or adolescence, when you were told, felt, or sensed that something about you was different, wrong, shameful, or unacceptable compared to other people. Perhaps you grew up in abject poverty and felt ashamed of your upbringing. Or maybe you were bullied at home or school for having learning or developmental disorders. It's also possible that your parents never felt satisfied with you and were difficult to please or abusive. These painful childhood experiences caused you to remove yourself from being at the center of your life and give other people or physical accomplishments (e.g., status, money, power) more attention and importance.

It is impossible to break free from the cycle of codependency without challenging this strong, negative belief, and the best way to challenge the belief is to cultivate self-love. Showing love for yourself is all the evidence you need to prove that you are worthy of affection, compassion, and support. It also sends a strong message to your inner critic and other people that you don't need anybody to complete your life story. You complete yourself.

Self-love is a public act of defiance against every negative thought that makes you feel insignificant and every manipulative person who makes you feel small. Your focus is not on proving to anybody that you are worthy but instead on actively investing in yourself and appreciating who you are. In other words, your value becomes recognizable to others not by what you have or how you come across in public but by how you take care of yourself, nurture your mind and body, invest in your personal development, and become obsessed with living a meaningful life.

Practicing self-love will feel foreign to you, especially if you have spent most of your life feeding into the belief that you are not good enough and that you need others to complete you. Nevertheless, you can learn to develop self-love by shifting your focus away from how society views you and onto how you view yourself. The contents of this chapter will guide you through the process and equip you with simple strategies to help you get started.

Unconditional Self-Love in its Truest Form

There is a difference between self-esteem and self-worth. Having high self-esteem means that you display confidence that comes from being skilled, talented, or successful at particular things in your life. For example, you could be a great singer and enjoy talking about music or singing to others in public. You feel good about yourself within the context of expressing your talent because you have above-average competence.

Self-esteem is context-based and subject to fluctuation whenever you feel on top of your game. Someone who derives their self-esteem from their career will feel confident for as long as they are getting promotions and climbing up the corporate ladder. When the promotions end, or they experience challenges at work, their self-esteem will drop, and they may start criticizing themselves or making comparisons with others who are seemingly more successful.

Self-worth is not related to self-esteem. We can define self-worth as the belief that there is value inside of you without having to add or improve anything about yourself. In other words, without developing skills, improving your appearance, picking up new hobbies, or forming new relationships, you are convinced that you are already worthy. All of the efforts you make to upgrade your life are done to enhance who you already are instead of transforming you into someone whom you believe others can trust, respect, and love.

It is easier to cultivate self-esteem than self-worth because the former is based on obtaining achievements, while the latter is based on your belief system and the amount of work you have done to address how you perceive yourself. Riding on your self-esteem works in the short term when you are excelling and everything is going well in your life. However, when you go through difficult life circumstances or when you find yourself having to express your needs or set boundaries in relationships, your self-worth is what protects you from being caught up in cycles of negative thinking, lowering your standards, and tolerating mistreatment from others.

Building a strong sense of self-worth requires loving yourself unconditionally, meaning without any disclaimers or expectations. From a young age, society has conditioned you to believe that the amount of respect you deserve is connected to how much work you have done to earn it. The same goes for love; you were told that love comes with sacrifices or that love doesn't come cheap. There were certain things that you needed to do to receive affection from others, and failure to do these things meant that you were not worthy of receiving affection.

Unconditional self-love flips this idea upside down and tells you that you are enough. Who you are today, with all the checkboxes that you have ticked or haven't ticked, is deserving of respect and affection. Unconditional self-love is not based on external merits like accomplishing goals, being liked by others, or having a good reputation. Instead, it is based on what you believe about yourself and what you are willing to do to live a meaningful life.

Having high self-esteem is not wrong, but it also shouldn't be what informs your thoughts and feelings about yourself. If everything that you owned or accomplished was taken away from you in an instant, would there still be a 'you' left behind? Or has your identity become so wrapped up in your career, finances, and relationships that you would be lost without them?

Practical Strategies to Develop Unconditional Self-Love

The goal of unconditional self-love is to let go of the burden of living for others and start living for yourself. But to do this, you need to sincerely believe that you are worth living for. Here are some practical strategies that can help you develop unconditional self-love:

1. **Enjoy moments of solitude:**

Learn to enjoy your own company and be content without human interaction. Moments of solitude, when taken within reasonable limits, can be opportunities to hear and affirm your thoughts and feelings. Your personality is so expansive that you cannot fully discover who you are through encounters with others. Some aspects of your personality are discovered through journaling, praying, meditating, or engaging in solo activities.

2. **Make your needs your priority:**

Take responsibility for how you feel by proactively addressing your needs. Don't wait for others to notice or volunteer to respond to your needs. For example, you might need a lot more affection from your partner than what they are providing. Instead of waiting for them to notice your discontent, you can take action and find ways to make yourself feel loved. This could be as simple as switching up your routine to make time for self-care practices or focusing on your personal development.

3. **Challenge your inner critic:**

Your inner critic is the voice of self-doubt that causes you to second-guess yourself. It is only as powerful as the attention you give to it. When you stop taking what it says about you seriously, you will notice that the negative thoughts become less intense and debilitating. Whenever you notice yourself being self-critical, acknowledge that your inner critic is inviting you to play a nasty game and decline the invitation. Continue with whatever train you thought you had before being interrupted.

4. **Decide how you want to feel about yourself:**

Oftentimes, we leave it up to other people to define who we are. We wait for compliments and recognition from others to reflect on our strengths and talents. Part of developing unconditional love is learning how to validate yourself through intentional thoughts and feelings. At each moment of the day, you can decide how you want to feel about yourself by considering what thoughts or emotions would make you feel good about yourself. Ask yourself: What is it that I need to feel or hear from myself right now to feel content?

5. **Show respect for yourself:**

We teach others what we are willing to tolerate through the level of self-respect we demonstrate. Self-respect is about aligning your words with your actions. Through your behaviors, you set invisible standards that communicate who you are and how you desire to be treated. When you respect yourself, you enforce clear boundaries and consequences that are grounded in principles, not emotions or familiarity. In other words, despite how much you love your romantic partner, there are certain things that you wouldn't allow them to get away with because you respect yourself.

6. **Embrace your quirks and differences:**

There could be certain qualities about yourself that don't fit the description of who others think you are. Maybe you have a quirky or playful side that you hide out of fear that you would lose favor with people if they saw it. While you have every right to reserve aspects of your personality for specific settings and people, it is important to acknowledge that you have these quirks and differences and that there is nothing wrong, taboo, or inappropriate about them. Set aside some time to explore your quirks and differences through hobbies, traveling, or connecting with like-minded people.

7. **Surround yourself with positive people:**

People can only treat you as well as they treat themselves. Being around negative people can cause you to develop new fears and insecurities due to the conversations and attitudes of the people around you. They may also sense your positive spirit and feel threatened, which would make them project their unwanted emotions onto you. When you surround yourself with positive people, you get to feed off the high energy of those around you and invest in relationships that are inspiring and positively contribute to your personal development.

How you talk to yourself influences how you feel about yourself. Self-talk refers to the ongoing dialogue that replays in the background of your mind while you are engaging with life. When your self-talk is negative, you tend to experience life through a negative filter and focus on your limitations or failures. However, when your self-talk is positive, you tend to experience life through a positive filter and focus on your strengths and hidden possibilities.

The following exercise will help you identify negative self-talk and switch to positive self-talk through four simple steps:

Step 1: Identify a Negative Self-Talk Trap

There are certain situations that you frequently come across that trigger negative self-talk. It might be feeling under pressure at work, having to communicate your needs to your partner, or receiving criticism from a family member. Make a note of these situations and describe when and how they happen, as well as how the self-talk dialogue normally goes. Here is an example:

Situation: My partner expresses a concern about our relationship.

When it happens: Whenever they feel unhappy.

How does it happen: They ask to have a chat with me and share their concerns.

Self-talk dialogue: I blame myself for not recognizing my partner's needs and responding accordingly. I feel like I have failed them and won't be able to fix the situation. I have questions about whether they will leave me or lose some of their affection for me.

Step 2: Challenge Your Negative Self-Talk

Focus on the self-talk dialogue that is triggered whenever the situation occurs. Work through each sentence and analyze the validity of your thoughts. The aim is not to judge yourself for thinking this way but instead to prove to yourself that your thoughts are based on negative assumptions and beliefs rather than facts. The following questions will help you challenge your negative self-talk:

- Are your thoughts based on logical conclusions or emotions?
- Do you know these statements as facts, or could you be guessing?
- Would a friend in your position interpret the situation in the same way?
- Do your thoughts match the reality of your situation or what you fear?
- Are your beliefs based on what is happening now or what happened in the past?

____

____

____

____

____

____

____

____

____

Step 3: Interrupt and Replace Your Negative Self-Talk

If you have found your self-talk dialogue to be emotion-based, full of assumptions, and based on your fears of the past repeating itself, then you can interrupt your pattern of thinking and replace your negative self-talk with positive self-talk. This entails looking at the triggering situation with a new set of eyes without being influenced by your pre-existing beliefs.

Reframe the dialogue and write it out in a manner that is fair, balanced, and matches reality. It doesn't need to be dramatically positive (otherwise, it wouldn't match reality); however, it must consider the fact that you are human and won't always behave perfectly. Here is an example of a rewritten dialogue using the example we started with:

Old self-talk dialogue: I blame myself for not recognizing my partner's needs and responding accordingly. I feel like I have failed them and won't be able to fix the situation. I have questions about whether they will leave me or lose some of their affection for me.

New self-talk dialogue: I made a mistake by not recognizing what my partner needed from me. By sharing their concerns with me, they are allowing me to make things right. My partner loves me and wants to work on our relationship. Otherwise, they would've shut me out. Now that I know what to avoid and what to do differently next time, we can both continue to build our relationship and make each other happy.

____

____

____

____

____

____

Step 4: Create Self-Affirming Statements to Support Your New Perspective

It is crucial to repeat the new self-talk dialogue over and over again to convince your mind to adopt the new perspective. Of course, when a similar situation occurs in the future, you will be tempted to go back to the old way of thinking. Having a few self-affirming statements and reciting them to yourself can help you calm your anxious mind and remember to think positively.

Based on your new self-talk dialogue, create self-affirming statements that support this positive way of thinking. Whenever you repeat the dialogue in your mind, recite your self-affirmations, too. Think of this as "supporting evidence" to back your new thoughts and beliefs about the situation. Self-affirming statements are positive phrases written in the present tense that help you perceive situations as you desire them to be. Examples of self-affirming statements include:

- I am a loving partner. My intentions are always good.
- I am continuously learning and becoming a better person.
- I deserve healthy and fulfilling relationships.
- I can use my strengths to come out of any situation.
- I embrace my fears, but I won't allow them to hold me back.
- Stepping out of my comfort zone takes courage, and I am proud of myself.
- I define myself and choose how I want to be seen in the world.

____

____

____

____

Small Acts of Smart Selfishness

A common codependency behavior is saying "yes" to plans or tasks when you meant or felt like saying "no." This happens when you feel pressured to give a specific response (e.g., when a coworker places work on your desk and says it's urgent) or when you don't want to disappoint the other person.

To keep yourself from being overly helpful, supportive, or kind, it is important to first delay giving a response. You are not forced to respond immediately to others' needs. Check-in with yourself and assess whether you have the capacity (i.e., time, energy, willpower, money, etc.) to offer assistance. Consider whether you have other pressing issues that require your time and energy.

This act of self-love is known as smart selfishness, and it involves honoring your needs and well-being for the long-term benefit of your relationships. Smart selfishness is not being neglectful of others but rather setting personal limits to avoid putting others first and creating a power imbalance. Remember, for relationships to function healthily, there must be a healthy dynamic of give-and-take. Therefore, sometimes, you need to hold back (even when you could do more) to allow others to also pour into you.

We have already discussed one example of smart selfishness, which is delaying giving a response and checking in with yourself. Some of the other ways you can practice smart selfishness include:

- Be selective about which invitations you honor and which you decline.
- Be selective about how much of your personal life you share with others.
- Take time off work to rest and replenish your energy.
- Avoid work calls, texts, or emails after work hours or on weekends.
- Avoid gossiping or having conversations that require too much emotional labor.

- Listen to a loved one vent their frustration without offering advice.
- Have a limit on how much money you are willing to borrow from others.
- Have a limit on how many times you will respond to favors or requests.
- Stop offering help when your efforts are not recognized or make a difference.
- Limit interactions with negative friends, family members, and coworkers.

You may feel guilt when practicing smart selfishness, but remember that you are responsible for taking care of yourself, not other people's needs. The time, energy, and support that you lavishly offer others should first assist you in achieving your goals and improving your life. After your needs are taken care of, you can then make yourself available to assist other people.

When you adopt this mindset in relationships, and your partner, friends, or relatives do the same, there is less stress and pressure piled on top of one another. Instead of being dependent on each other for survival, you can be interdependent and focus on bigger goals, like how to build and strengthen your relationships.

The New and Complete You

Throughout the book, you have been taken through various strategies to end the dysfunctional cycle of give-and-take in your relationships that has caused power imbalances.

All of the strategies you have been introduced to, such as shifting from enabler to caregiver, overcoming the fear of abandonment, letting go of people-pleasing tendencies, and setting boundaries, have helped you focus on your well-being, prioritize your needs, and actively build the type of relationships that you desire.

Congratulations on getting this far into the "Complete You" journey. The valuable skills and strategies you have learned thus far are already in full effect and slowly transforming how you view and approach relationships. You may not notice the behavioral changes immediately since they begin on a subconscious level. However, don't let that stop you from practicing the tools you have learned.

It is never easy to confront toxic patterns and behaviors because the process can be somewhat intimidating. You should be proud of yourself for keeping an open mind and heart throughout the journey and willingly confronting your relationship dynamics. Codependency cannot be fixed overnight but through an ongoing determination to think and behave differently in your relationships. The good news is that along this journey, you have discovered the 'New and Complete You' who will support you in bringing a complete end to the codependency cycle!

10.

Bonus Chapter: From Drama to Empowerment—Your Complete Transformation

You'll learn, as you get older, that rules are made to be broken. Be bold enough to live life on your terms, and never, ever apologize for it. Go against the grain, refuse to conform, take the road less traveled instead of the well-beaten path. Laugh in the face of adversity, and leap before you look. –Mandy Hale

"

Celebrating Your Personal Transformation

You have successfully gone through the Complete You blueprint and made progress in ending the cycle of codependency in your relationships. This bonus chapter has been added to further enhance your personal transformation by showing you an illustration of where you come from and where you are possibly heading.

In Chapter 1, you were introduced to the Karpman Drama Triangle, which consisted of three interconnected roles: rescuer, victim, and persecutor. In your codependent relationships, you often switch between these roles depending on your circumstances. Falling into the Karpman Drama Triangle trap partly contributed to the dysfunctional pattern of give-and-take. Now that you are no longer a prisoner of your past relationship behaviors, you can adopt new and healthy dynamics in your relationships.

The purpose of this chapter is to show you the inverse of the Karpman Drama Triangle called the Empowerment Triangle, which you can set as your goal as you learn and practice positive ways to relate to others.

The Empowerment Triangle

The Empowerment Triangle is a concept created by Dr. Stephen Karpman, the same man who invented the Karpman Drama Triangle. It breaks away from the unfair and conflictual Drama Triangle, where there is an imbalance of give-and-take, and seeks to provide a positive alternative that fosters compassion, constructive feedback, and creative problem-solving.

To appreciate the Empowerment Triangle, it is important to refresh yourself on the Karpman Drama Triangle. In summary, three roles are common to find in codependent relationships: rescuer, victim, and persecutor. The rescuer attempts to fix or change what isn't working in the relationship by being overly helpful, a people-pleaser, or enabling the inappropriate behaviors of others. The victim struggles to express their thoughts and feelings and, therefore, rarely gets their needs met. They feel unheard and powerless in the relationship and are always waiting for someone to recognize and respond to their needs.

The persecutor seeks control in the relationship and tends to blame others (i.e., the victim and rescuer) for not doing enough to solve problems and address relationship challenges. In many cases, the persecutor is a narcissistic partner, friend, or coworker. However, codependent people can become persecutors once they have grown tired of suppressing their needs and being taken for granted in their relationships.

In your various relationships, you might play different roles. For example, at work, you may play the role of a persecutor because you tried people-pleasing and found that your colleagues took advantage of your kindness. To get work done, you rule with an iron fist and enforce strict boundaries. However, in your romantic relationship, you play the role of a victim and find excuses for not communicating your needs, setting healthy boundaries, and speaking up for yourself. Instead of presenting your concerns and having a discussion with your partner about them, you might downplay the severity of the problem and pretend nothing is wrong.

The Empowerment Triangle aims to get you out of this unfulfilling dynamic by switching roles. Here is a look at how the rescuer, victim, and persecutor transform into the coach, creator, and challenger:

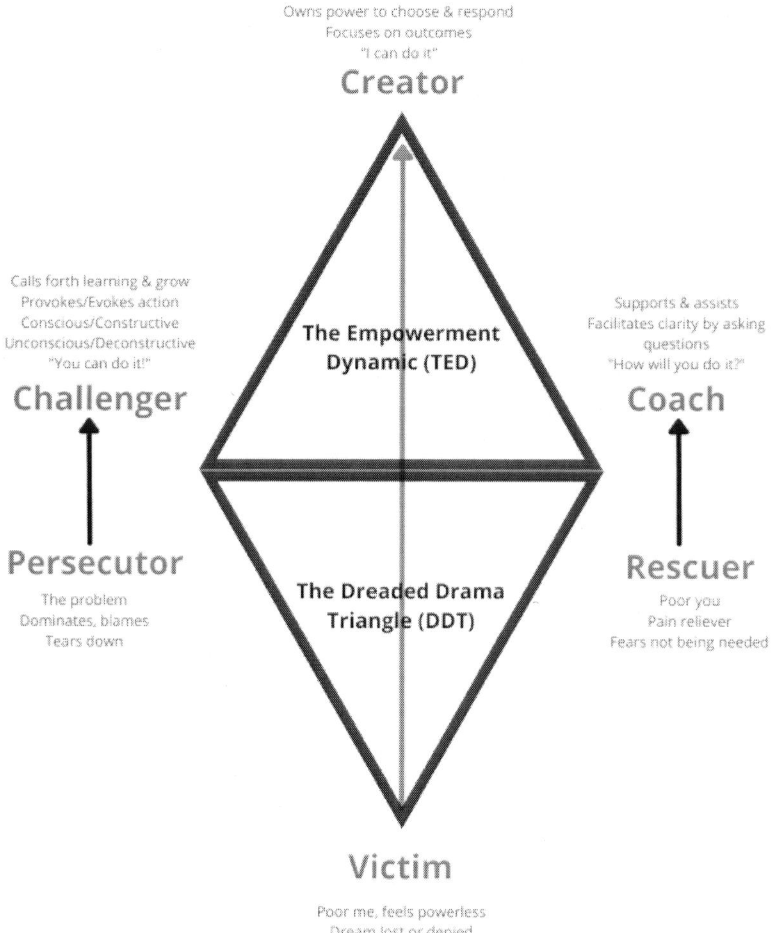

From Rescuer to Coach

If you identify as a rescuer, you feel good about yourself when helping other people. However, as you know, sometimes being too helpful and overextending yourself can cause unbalanced relationships where you enable bad behavior or do more emotional labor than others.

To protect your interests while remaining a dedicated caregiver, you can transition to a coach. The role of a coach is not to do the work for people but instead to offer support and encouragement while they solve their own problems and play an active role in shaping their own lives. Being a coach means taking a step back and being less hands-on. This also means allowing people to experience challenges and failures without stepping in to rescue them.

For example, a mother who is a rescuer might decide to take a step back from overparenting their teenager and allow them to experience the challenges that come with adolescence on their own. They aren't completely neglecting their child but rather supporting from the sidelines and offering guidance when necessary. Their child, who may have felt like a victim, gets to contend with life on their own terms and develop the confidence and independence required to be a stable adult.

From Victim to Creator

If you identify as a victim, you do not feel like you have control of your life. You often blame others for not responding to your needs or playing a part in making the relationship work. The fear or struggle to express your honest thoughts and feelings means that you internalize your frustrations and harbor secret resentment toward the people who fail to recognize and respond to your needs.

To put an end to the chronic feeling of being powerless in your relationships, you can transition to a creator. The role of a creator is to take action in shaping their lives and relationships. The creator doesn't wait for a thumbs up before leaping forward and making changes within their control. They develop confidence by doing rather than speaking about what they can do. Being a creator means acknowledging that you always have a choice in your relationships and taking measures to solve problems, one step at a time.

For example, a mother who is a rescuer might decide to take a step back from overparenting their teenager and allow them to experience the challenges that come with adolescence on their own. They aren't completely neglecting their child but rather supporting them from the sidelines and offering guidance when necessary. Their child, who may have felt like a victim, gets to contend with life on their own terms and develop the confidence and independence required to be a stable adult.

From Persecutor to Challenger

If you identify as a persecutor, you have gotten so tired of being abused and manipulated in your relationships that you have become rigid. Similar to the victim, you struggle to communicate your needs in healthy ways, so you end up passing blame, criticizing, and enforcing strict boundaries. All of this is done to get the attention of others and hopefully convince them to respond to your needs.

Being dominant in your relationships may cause you to be perceived as a bully, even though that may not be your intention. To be assertive without turning aggressive, you can transition to a challenger. The role of a challenger is to pave the way for others by showing them who they could be or how they could show up differently in their relationships. Instead of pushing others to do what they may not feel comfortable doing, you can set a vision and inspire them to follow it. In some way, you also take on the role of creator by setting standards and living by them.

For example, a wife may feel frustrated with her husband's eating habits. Criticizing his diet and demanding that he adopt a healthier lifestyle hasn't worked over the years; it has only made him emotionally shut down and turn to food for comfort. By taking on the role of a challenger, she can set a vision for a healthier family and inspire her husband to follow the vision through encouragement.

This would require her full commitment first, which can be seen through changes to her diet, fitness regimen, sleep routine, stress management, and overall self-care practices. The positive results she saw in her life would motivate her husband to take an interest in adopting a healthier lifestyle. Even if her husband decides not to follow the new lifestyle, she has found better ways to channel her frustrations—through making positive changes to her own life.

EXERCISE

Transitioning From the Karpman Drama Triangle to the Empowerment Triangle

The following exercise provides a step-by-step guide on how to transition from your current role on the Karpman Drama Triangle to the equivalent role on the Empowerment Triangle.

On the line space provided, answer the following reflection questions:

1. Describe a drama playing out in your life. Focus on a specific situation that is causing stress in one of the four relationships (e.g., romantic, family, social, and professional).

____

____

____

____

2. Weigh the costs and impact of this situation. For example, what are the ripple effects of the situation? Who will be affected? What are the long-term consequences for your health and well-being?

____

____

____

____

3. What are your main concerns about the situation? What are you focused on? What do you wish could happen?

4. What do you have the urge to do? What steps do you wish you could take? How do you want to address the situation?

5. How do you wish the other people involved in the situation could act? What steps do you desire them to take?

Based on your situation, identify which role in the Karpman Drama Triangle you are currently playing. Use the descriptions of the thoughts, emotions, and behaviors of each role to help you find the one you resonate with the most.

Role	Thoughts	Emotions	Behaviors	Personal comments
Victim	It's not my fault. No one cares. I am powerless.	Helpless Unsatisfied Neglected	Emotional Lack energy Complacent Gives up easily	
Persecutor	I need control. I know best. I am exploited.	Defensive Angry Misunderstood	Arrogance Criticism Compliance by force	
Rescuer	I need to save others. Giving support makes me worthy.	Fearful Guilty Exhausted	Self-sacrificing Enabling People-pleasing	

After you have identified your role, answer the following set of reflection questions:

6. Reflect on your earliest memory of entering this role. What life circumstances were you under at the time? What pressures were you facing?

7. What was the motivation for entering this particular role? What benefits could you get out of it? How did the role promise to improve your relationships?

8. What have been the drawbacks of being in this role? How has it negatively impacted your relationships? Who has this role prevented you from becoming?

Focus on the other two roles that you didn't pick and reflect on when and how you have stepped into them in the past.

1. **Role 1:** Reflect on a memory of you entering this role. What life circumstances were you under at the time? What pressures were you facing?

____

____

____

____

2. **Role 1:** What was the motivation for entering this particular role? What benefits could you get out of it? How did the role promise to improve your relationships?

____

____

____

____

3. **Role 1:** What have been the drawbacks of being in this role? How has it negatively impacted your relationships? Who has this role prevented you from becoming?

____

____

____

____

4. **Role 2:** Reflect on a memory of you entering this role. What life circumstances were you under at the time? What pressures were you facing?

---

5. **Role 2:** What was the motivation for entering this particular role? What benefits could you get out of it? How did the role promise to improve your relationships?

---

6. **Role 2:** What have been the drawbacks of being in this role? How has it negatively impacted your relationships? Who has this role prevented you from becoming?

Refer back to the original role you identified in Questions 6–8 and answer the following questions to begin transitioning from the Karpman Drama Triangle to the Empowerment Triangle.

1. Recall the drama that you outlined at the beginning of this exercise and reflect on how you handled the situation. Things to consider include:

    - What were you thinking about?
    - What did you keep saying to yourself?
    - Were your actions outcome-oriented?

2. How did you interact with others?

___

___

___

___

___

3. Now that you have more knowledge about the situation, determine three things that you have learned and what you would do differently.

___

___

___

___

___

Based on your insights, identify which role in the Empowerment Triangle fits your current mindset and attitude. Use the descriptions of the thoughts, emotions, and behaviors of each role to help you find the one you resonate with the most.

Role	Thoughts	Emotions	Behaviors	Personal comments
Creator	I have a choice. I am focused on what I can change.	Energized Optimistic Resilient	Problem-solver Innovative Goal-oriented	
Challenger	Trust the process. I believe in you.	Inspired Confident Focused	Accountable Leadership Motivational	
Coach	People are resilient. I empathize without taking on your problems.	Engaged Self-aware Supportive but detached	Curiosity Positive reinforcement Encouragement	

After you have identified your role, answer the following set of reflection questions:

1. Think of someone you know who has adopted this role. What type of beliefs do they have regarding relationships? How do they interact with other people?

____

____

____

2. Create a list of values of someone who embodies this role. Think of at least five values they possess and demonstrate in their relationships.

3. Create a list of boundaries for someone who embodies this role. Think of at least five different boundaries they would set when entering a relationship.

4. What baby steps can you take today to start showing up in your new role? Make a list of small tasks or behaviors you can adopt to reset your mindset and approach relationships differently.

____

____

____

____

____

5. Here are a few practical tips on how you can transition to the Empowerment Triangle roles:

From Victim to Creator

- Listen to the language you use. Replace phrases like "I have to" or "I should" with "I choose to" and "I want to." This slight change reminds you that you have a choice.
- Focus on things that you have the power to change. There may not be many, but directing your energy toward them can boost your confidence and inspire action.
- Consider grey areas instead of seeing situations as being black or white. Practice looking at situations from different perspectives and considering the fears or challenges others may be faced with.
- Practice positive affirmations to combat negative thinking and focus on what you desire or hope for instead of the current problem.
- Surround yourself with creators and challengers who can affirm your strengths and positively influence your behaviors.

From Persecutor to Challenger

- Train your brain to look for "what's right" instead of "what's wrong" with other people. Practice the 5:1 ratio rule. For every negative, find five positives.

- Give yourself a break. Cultivate self-compassion and practice talking to yourself like you would a friend. Remind yourself that you are only human and doing the best you can.

- Look for teachable moments in every circumstance. Ask yourself, "What has this situation taught me?" Continue to invest in your personal growth and learning.

- Influence others by being the change you desire to see. Become intentional about living a purposeful life full of rich experiences and meaningful relationships.

- Create a belief and value system that gives your life a sense of direction. Use this system as the foundation for your interactions with others. Set boundaries to ensure that your relationships mirror your beliefs and values.

From Rescuer to Coach

- Learn to respect other people's boundaries and step back when you sense resistance.

- Encourage others to take responsibility for their lives instead of being dependent on your assistance.

- Listen and ask questions like, "What do you think needs to happen?" instead of being quick to solve other people's problems.

- Learn to say no to requests that demand too much time or energy from you.

- Provide positive reinforcement, like praising progress when others show signs of independence or proactive problem-solving.

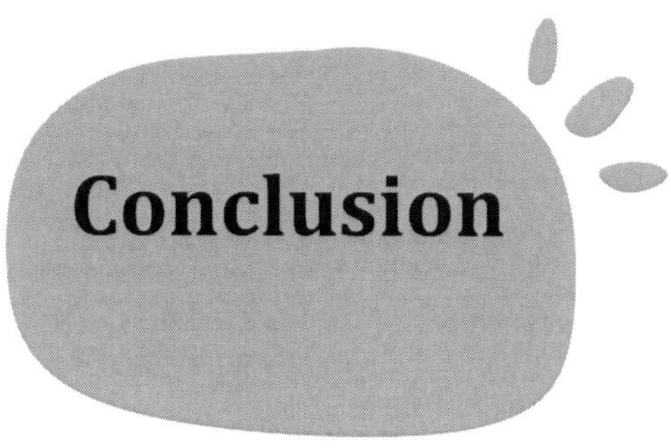

Somehow, we'll find it. The balance between whom we wish to be and whom we need to be. But for now, we simply have to be satisfied with who we are. –Brandon Sanderson

Reflecting on Your Journey Thus Far

Codependency may not be a medical condition, but it is a serious behavioral pattern that can negatively impact how you explore and navigate relationships. You cannot escape the fact that you need people in your life, whether it is as family, friends, colleagues, or romantic partners. However, how you approach relationships can either support or compromise your mental and emotional well-being.

The content of this book was framed around the Complete You blueprint, which comprises various strategies that can help you achieve balance, wholeness, and satisfaction within yourself. The core message behind this framework is that prioritizing your needs and showing yourself the love, admiration, and support you desire from others can promote a healthy sense of self and give you the confidence to be bold and unapologetic about who you are.

Throughout your life, you have struggled to find your voice, articulate your needs, or set healthy boundaries with others. The significance of reading this book is that those issues have been left behind in the past. Over ten chapters, you have been presented with different types of psychological skills and tools that are effective in regaining lost aspects of your identity, addressing trauma-related coping mechanisms, and redefining relationships on your terms.

You have all of the resources necessary to analyze each of your relationships through a microscope and identify behavioral red flags, dysfunctional give-and-take cycles, and serious boundary violations that need appropriate consequences. The days of being mistreated and taken for granted are over because the New and Complete You has stepped into the building!

From Codependency to Interdependency

Now that you have an empowered outlook on your life, where does that leave your relationships? The unique challenge you are presented with is to allow your relationships to evolve from a place of codependency to a place of interdependency by lovingly detaching from others enough to see them as their own persons.

As you close the chapter of your life marked with codependency and open a new chapter of interdependency, your ongoing task is to celebrate what makes you and others unique. You have the potential to inspire others with your life story and add so much value to your relationships by showing up as your authentic self. Your differences are what draw people to you and make you unforgettable. Celebrate your individuality and create room for others to express themselves freely around you, too!

Embrace each day as an opportunity to take care of yourself for the long-term benefit of your relationships. Enjoy the process of learning and practicing healthier patterns, as well as teaching your loved ones how to relate to you and speak your love languages. Indeed, there will be a lot of learning and unlearning involved in rewriting the narrative of your relationships. See this as an opportunity to reintroduce yourself to others and become who you have always desired to be.

The journey of ending the codependency cycle is long and tedious, so give yourself breaks and appreciate the progress you make on a day-to-day basis. These small victories add up and fuel the motivation to continue on your path toward greater self-love and independence.

Share Your Experience

Congratulations on completing your journey through the Codependency Recovery Workbook! Now that you have armed yourself with essential tools to manage and recover from codependency, it's time to share your newfound wisdom.

By leaving your honest review of this book on Amazon, you're not just offering feedback; you're guiding other readers who are seeking the same transformation. You have the power to direct them to the help they need and to pass along the passion for recovery that this workbook ignites.

Your review plays a crucial role in keeping the life-changing message of the Codependency Recovery Workbook vibrant and alive. By sharing your experience, you help ensure that others can find this resource and start their own journey of healing and growth.

Thank you for your invaluable contribution. Your support keeps this workbook thriving and continues the cycle of knowledge and healing.

Please, scan the QR code to leave your review:

Together, we're not just reading a book; we're creating a community of awareness, recovery, and mindfulness. Thanks to you, this important work continues. Let's keep the game alive!

With deepest appreciation, Lulu Nicholson

PS - Did you know? Sharing something of value with another person enriches both of your lives. If you believe this book could illuminate someone else's path, consider passing it along.

References

Abraham, A. (2019, December 5). *Unconditional self-love: 10 practical ways to love yourself unconditionally*. The Soul Jam. https://www.thesouljam.com/post/10-practical-ways-towards-unconditional-self-love

Albright, M. K. (n.d.). *Madeleine K. Albright quote*. Goodreads. https://www.goodreads.com/author/show/63111.Madeleine_K_Albright

Andrade, S. (2021, July 1). *Council post: The importance of setting healthy boundaries*. Forbes. https://www.forbes.com/sites/forbescoachescouncil/2021/07/01/the-importance-of-setting-healthy-boundaries/?sh=7396afcf56e4

Anotherdangbreakup. (2021, June 21). *So, I think i'm codependent. my story and a "what now?"* Reddit. https://www.reddit.com/r/Codependency/comments/o507mu/so_i_think_im_codependent_my_story_and_a_what_now/

Askew, C. (2015). *How to process emotions and feelings*. Recovery from Addiction Online. https://www.recoveryfromaddictiononline.com/how-to-process-emotions-and-feelings/

Attachment styles and their role in our adult relationships. (2020, July 2). Attachment Project. https://www.attachmentproject.com/blog/four-attachment-styles/

Beattie, M. (2022, September 11). *Best +35 codependency quotes every codependent needs to read*. Ineffable Living. https://ineffableliving.com/codependency-quotes/

Beattie, M. (n.d.). *Codependent no more quotes by Melody Beattie*. Goodreads. https://www.goodreads.com/work/quotes/706540-codependent-no-more-how-to-stop-controlling-others-and-start-caring-for

Bradstreet, C. (2019, January 1). *Use the power of release to heal yourself*. Change Your Mind Change Your Life. https://medium.com/change-your-mind/you-can-use-the-power-of-release-to-heal-yourself-c08abc70c890

Brady, K. (2019, June 5). *Five types of boundaries for your relationship.* Keir Brady Counseling. https://keirbradycounseling.com/relationship-boundaries/

Brown, B. (n.d.). *Brené Brown quote.* Goodreads. https://www.goodreads.com/author/show/162578.Bren_Brown

Buffybot3000. (2021, December 29). *Struggling with fears of abandonment the more I like my partner.* Reddit. https://www.reddit.com/r/AskWomenOver30/comments/rqzoy9/struggling_with_fears_of_abandonment_the_more_i/

Bunch, E. (2020, July 9). *Are you an enabler? Here's how to tell and—more importantly—six tips to stop.* Well and Good. https://www.wellandgood.com/how-to-stop-enabling/

Chesak, J. (2021, May 6). *The no BS guide to mastering unwanted emotions.* Healthline. https://www.healthline.com/health/mental-health/developing-self-awareness#write-your-way-to-change

Chrysalis Courses. (2019). *Why communication is key to relationships.* Chrysalis Courses. https://www.chrysaliscourses.ac.uk/news/why-communication-is-key-to-healthy-relationships

Cikanavicius, D. (2017, August 28). *The trap of external validation for self-esteem.* Psych Central. https://psychcentral.com/blog/psychology-self/2017/08/validation-self-esteem#1

Codependency triangle in narcissistic relationships. (2021, December 8). Grace Being. https://grace-being.com/love-relationships/codependency-triangle-in-narcissistic-relationships/

Conflict management with teenagers. (2021, September 8). Raising Children Network. https://raisingchildren.net.au/teens/communicating-relationships/communicating/conflict-management-with-teens

Dawn, M. (2020, November 16). *How to set healthy boundaries in difficult (and all) times.* CEO of Your Life. https://ceoofyour.life/2020/11/how-to-set-healthy-boundaries-in-difficult-and-all-times/

Deschene, L. (2023, January 17). *Fifty codependency quotes for relationship clarity*. Everyday Power. https://everydaypower.com/codependency-quotes/

Elkassih, B. (2022, October 17). *The top traits about a caring personality*. Made You Smile Back. https://madeyousmileback.com/the-top-traits-of-a-caring-personality/

Emerald, D. (2015). *Making the shift from drama to empowerment*. Fosteractionohio. https://fosteractionohio.files.wordpress.com/2019/02/power-of-ted.pdf

Fabian, S. (2018, June 25). *Five practices that helped me stop being a people-pleaser*. Tiny Buddha. https://tinybuddha.com/blog/5-practices-helped-me-stop-being-a-people-pleaser/

Geiger, M. R. (2023, May 8). *Communication in relationships: Why is it so hard?* Miriam Geiger. https://miriamgeiger.com/communication-in-relationships/

Glass, L. J. (2023, October 13). *Four stages of enabling behavior in relationships*. Love to Pivot. https://www.lovetopivot.com/what-stages-enabling-behavior-four-types-enabler/

Gooden, A. (2020, November 18). *How to cultivate a sense of unconditional self-worth*. Ideas TED. https://ideas.ted.com/how-to-cultivate-a-sense-of-unconditional-self-worth/

Grant, R. (n.d.). *Overcome the fear of abandonment*. Rachel Grant Coaching. https://www.rachelgrantcoaching.com/media/abandonment.pdf

Green, R. (2023, April 27). *How to live with authenticity and be your truest self*. Verywell Mind. https://www.verywellmind.com/live-with-authenticity-7483232

Hailey, L. (n.d.). *How to set boundaries: 5 Ways to draw the line politely*. Science of People. https://www.scienceofpeople.com/how-to-set-boundaries/

Hale, M. (2023, November 10). *Thirty+ self love quotes to boost your self-esteem*. Earthraga. https://www.earthraga.com/blogs/news/30-self-love-quotes-to-boost-your-self-esteem

Hale, M. (n.d.). *Mandy Hale quote*. Goodreads. https://www.goodreads.com/author/show/5623882.Mandy_Hale

Hambrick, B. (2016, October 17). *Strategies for overcoming codependency: Building resilience (2 of 3)*. Brad Hambrick. https://bradhambrick.com/strategies-for-overcoming-codependency-building-resilience-2-of-3/

How to actually feel your feelings: a guide to processing your emotions. (2023, July 5).. Calm Blog. https://www.calm.com/blog/how-to-feel-your-feelings

Indeed Editorial Team. (2022, September 15). *What is co-dependency in the workplace? (with common signs)*. Indeed. https://au.indeed.com/career-advice/career-development/co-dependency-in-work-place

Jones, C. T. (n.d.). *Curtis Tyrone Jones quote*. Goodreads. https://www.goodreads.com/author/show/6023661.Curtis_Tyrone_Jones

Joye, M. (2020, September 1). *The extremes of the codependency spectrum and how to gain balance*. Thrive Global. https://community.thriveglobal.com/the-extremes-of-the-codependency-spectrum-and-how-to-gain-balance/

Keen, S. (n.d.). *Sam Keen quote*. Goodreads. https://www.goodreads.com/author/show/178984.Sam_Keen

Kerkez, Y. (2023, March 5). *How to recognize if you are existing in a codependent family relationship*. Codependency Recovery Council. https://codependencyrecovery.org/2023/03/05/how-to-recognize-if-you-are-existing-in-a-codependent-family-relationship/

Klotz-Guest, K. (2016, April 5). *The authenticity paradox and life lessons learned from a (mostly) reformed people-pleaser*. Medium. https://kathyklotzguest.medium.com/the-authenticity-paradox-and-life-lessons-learned-from-a-mostly-reformed-people-pleaser-3ec1d9648a27

Kohli, S. (2020, February 24). *Come, fall in love with yourself by taking these 7 steps to unconditional self love.* Healthshots. https://www.healthshots.com/mind/emotional-health/take-these-7-steps-to-practice-unconditional-self-love/

Kraska, A. (2019, February 22). *How to stop being an enabler.* South Coast Behavioral Health. https://www.scbh.com/how-to-stop-being-an-enabler/

Lancer, D. (2023, October 20). *The spectrum of codependency.* Dummies. https://www.dummies.com/article/body-mind-spirit/emotional-health-psychology/psychology/diagnoses/codependency/the-spectrum-of-codependency-144336/

Lobel, D. S. (2022, November 13). *Three tools for coping with abandonment and the fear of abandonment.* Psychology Today. https://www.psychologytoday.com/intl/blog/my-side-the-couch/202211/3-tools-coping-abandonment-and-the-fear-abandonment

Lockett, E. (2022, October 20). *What is a codependent relationship? Could I be in one?* Healthline. https://www.healthline.com/health/relationships/codependent-relationship#taker-signs

Loyd, R. (2018, March 20). *What it really means to love yourself unconditionally.* Tiny Buddha. https://tinybuddha.com/blog/unconditional-self-love-looks-like/

Lyons, M. (2021, September 7). *Being your authentic self is easier said than done but worth it.* BetterUp. https://www.betterup.com/blog/authentic-self

Madeson, M. (2023, August 15). *How to overcome fear of abandonment: Six helpful worksheets.* Positive Psychology. https://positivepsychology.com/fear-of-abandonment/#assessing-fear-of-abandonment-4-tests

Mae, E. (2023, June 19). *10 codependent journal prompts for self-reflection and healing.* Coloring Folder. https://coloringfolder.com/codependent-journal-prompts/

Manning-Schaffel, V. (2018, December 5). *What is codependency? Signs of a codependent relationship.* NBC News. https://www.nbcnews.com/better/health/what-codependency-signs-codependent-relationship-ncna940666

Margolies, L. (2019, November 16). *How to set boundaries with difficult people: Do's and don'ts.* Psych Central. https://psychcentral.com/lib/how-to-set-boundaries-with-difficult-people#Popular-mistakes-that-cause-boundary-setting-to-fail:

McGahan, K. (n.d.). *Fear of abandonment quotes (nine quotes).* Goodreads. https://www.goodreads.com/quotes/tag/fear-of-abandonment

Mead, E. (2019, September 26). *What is positive self-talk? (Incl. examples).* Positive Psychology. https://positivepsychology.com/positive-self-talk/#benefits

Moshfegh, N. (2024, January 12). *How to express your feelings in writing.* WikiHow. https://www.wikihow.com/Express-Your-Feelings-in-Writing

Moving from codependent to interdependent relationships. (2019, November 29). Gender & Sexuality Therapy Center. https://www.gstherapycenter.com/blog/2019/11/25/moving-from-codependent-to-interdependent-relationships

Nash, P. (2024, January 18). *10 personality traits that show you're a deeply caring person.* Hack Spirit. https://hackspirit.com/personality-traits-of-deeply-caring-person/

Nine tips for parenting with open communication. (2021, October 6). The Social Child. https://thesocialchild.com.au/9-tips-for-parenting-with-open-communication/

Ohlin, B. (2017, August 25). *Seven ways to improve communication in relationships.* Positive Psychology. https://positivepsychology.com/communication-in-relationships/#better-communication-relationships

Palms, P. F. (2022, October 17). *How do codependency and interdependency differ?* Promises Five Palms. https://www.my5palms.com/addiction-blog/how-do-codependency-and-interdependency-differ/

Parker, E. (2017, March 20). *Fourteen quotes to inspire you to ditch your people-pleasing ways.* Psych Central. https://psychcentral.com/blog/imperfect/2017/03/14-quotes-to-inspire-you-to-ditch-your-people-pleasing-ways#4

Perez, A. L. (2023, December 10). *Healthy boundaries worksheet and example.* Care Patron. https://www.carepatron.com/templates/healthy-boundaries-worksheet

Perry, E. (2022, December 21). *Self-Reflection: Learn how to better understand yourself.* BetterUp. https://www.betterup.com/blog/self-reflection

Philosophyofthemind. (2020, September 6). *Men, what are some of your examples of good communication in a relationship? Bad examples?* Reddit. https://www.reddit.com/r/AskMen/comments/inrd1a/men_what_are_some_of_your_examples_of_good/

Pietrangelo, A. (2019, February 13). *What is fear of abandonment, and can it be treated?* Healthline Media. https://www.healthline.com/health/fear-of-abandonment

Plattor, C. (2018, August 1). *Recovering from codependency: The truth about people-pleasing.* Medium. https://medium.com/@candaceplattor/recovering-from-codependency-the-truth-about-people-pleasing-6e41d8d5a8d7

Poligirl17. (2017, October 25). *Codependency-my story.* Reddit. https://www.reddit.com/r/Codependency/comments/78q7u0/codependency_my_story/

Potter, A. (2021, April 29). *Five codependency symptoms of an adult child and codependent parent.* Mill Creek Christian Counseling. https://millcreekchristiancounseling.com/5-codependency-symptoms-of-an-adult-child-and-codependent-parent/

Pugle, M. (2023, March 27). *Helping vs. enabling: What's the difference?* Psych Central. https://psychcentral.com/health/what-is-the-difference-between-supporting-and-enabling#understanding-enabling

Raypole, C. (2021, June 10). *Are you codependent? Here are the key signs of codependency*. Psych Central. https://psychcentral.com/lib/symptoms-signs-of-codependency#examples

Rebecca. (2023, August). *Fifteen essential ways to practice self-reflection*. Minimalism Made Simple. https://www.minimalismmadesimple.com/home/self-reflection/

Reid, S. (2023, March 1). *Setting healthy boundaries in relationships*. HelpGuide. https://www.helpguide.org/articles/relationships-communication/setting-healthy-boundaries-in-relationships.htm

Rice, M. (2022, September 20). *Exploring the fear of abandonment*. Talkspace. https://www.talkspace.com/blog/fear-of-abandonment/

Robinson, L., Segal, J., & Jaffe, J. (2021, February). *How attachment styles affect adult relationships*. HelpGuide. https://www.helpguide.org/articles/relationships-communication/attachment-and-adult-relationships.htm

Rosario, T. M. D. (2022, October 27). *The power of communication in a relationship*. Healing Collective Therapy. https://www.healingcollectivetherapy.com/resources/power-of-communication-in-relationship

Roth, G. (2023, January 17). *50 codependency quotes for relationship clarity*. Everyday Power. https://everydaypower.com/codependency-quotes/

Sachdev, G. (2022, January 10). *Why do some people need constant validation? An expert tells us all*. Health Shots. https://www.healthshots.com/mind/mental-health/need-for-validation-and-its-effects-on-mental-health/

Sanderson, B. (n.d.). *Brandon Sanderson quote*. Goodreads. https://www.goodreads.com/author/show/38550.Brandon_Sanderson

Santos-Longhurst, A. (2022, March 31). *How to identify your love language*. Healthline. https://www.healthline.com/health/love-languages#what-they-are

Schwegman, K. (2022, January 7). *Unhealthy communication habits to be aware of and how to respond*. Holistic Wellness Practice. https://www.holisticwellnesspractice.com/hwp-blog/2022/01/07/unhealthy-communication-habits-to-be-aware-of-how-to-respond-instead

Seaver, M. (2023, March 29). *5 mindfulness breathing exercises you can do anywhere, anytime*. Real Simple. https://www.realsimple.com/health/mind-mood/breathing-exercises

Serai, P. (2023, December 27). *Narcissistic supply: 34 secrets to control a narcissist and cut their power ASAP!* Love Panky. https://www.lovepanky.com/love-couch/better-love/narcissistic-supply

Smith, K. (2022, May 20). *Signs of a codependent vs. interdependent relationship*. Psych Central. https://psychcentral.com/lib/codependency-vs-interdependency

Smith, S. (2023, June 23). *The importance of communication in relationships*. Marriage. https://www.marriage.com/advice/communication/importance-of-communication-in-relationships/

Spider-ren00. (2021, April 17). *Struggling with fear of abandonment*. Reddit. https://www.reddit.com/r/infj/comments/msu8z9/struggling_with_fear_of_abandonment/

TED (*The Empowerment Dynamic)*. (2021, December 31). Center for the Empowerment Dynamic. https://theempowermentdynamic.com/about/

Telloian, C. (2021, November 5). *Four tips to overcome fear of abandonment*. Psych Central. https://psychcentral.com/

health/fear-of-abandonment#how-to-overcome

Ten toxic communication patterns that hurt relationships. (2022, March 29). Marriage. https://www.marriage.com/advice/communication/toxic-communication-patterns/

The drama triangle and the empowerment dynamic approach to conflict. (2022, March 9). The Profit Recipe. https://theprofitrecipe.com/blog/drama-triangle-and-empowerment-dynamic

The drama triangle explained. (2020, December 4). Leadership Tribe US. https://leadershiptribe.com/blog/the-drama-triangle-explained

The drama triangle worksheet [PDF]. (n.d.). https://static1.squarespace.com/static/5989b157c534a519616d84cb/t/5f6c04797d664f2c1f627727/1600914556775/THE+DRAMA+TRIANGLE+WORKSHEET.pdf

Tyack, D. (2023, May 9). *You complete me.* Daniel Tyack. https://danieltyack.com/you-complete-me/

Young, A. (2023, July 14). *The people-pleasing paradox - why it often leads to less love and respect.* Subconscious Servant. https://subconsciousservant.com/the-people-pleasing-paradox/

Yvainne94. (2020, February 9). *Long story about my codependent relationship, how it ended and feeling despair.* Reddit. https://www.reddit.com/r/Codependency/comments/f1a7yw/long_story_about_my_codependent_relationship_how/

Zajonc, D., & Womeldorff, D. E. (2021). *Three vital questions workbook.* https://learning.3vitalquestions.com/wp-content/uploads/2021/08/eCourse-Workbook-Interactive.pdf

Made in United States
North Haven, CT
18 August 2024

56243393R00087